Landmarks of world literature

Geoffrey Chaucer

THE CANTERBURY TALES

For Christina
All the things you
already know, I'm
afraid, but neatly
printed out.

Love,

Peter

Landmarks of world literature

General Editor: J. P. Stern

GEOFFREY CHAUCER

The Canterbury Tales

WINTHROP WETHERBEE

Professor, Departments of Classics and English, Cornell University

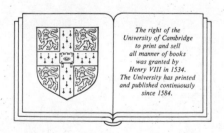

The right of the
University of Cambridge
to print and sell
all manner of books
was granted by
Henry VIII in 1534.
The University has printed
and published continuously
since 1584.

CAMBRIDGE UNIVERSITY PRESS

Cambridge

New York   Port Chester

Melbourne   Sydney

Published by the Press Syndicate of the University of Cambridge
The Pitt Building, Trumpington Street, Cambridge CB2 1RP
20 West 40th Street, New York, NY 10011, USA
10 Stamford Road, Oakleigh, Melbourne 3166, Australia

First published 1989

Printed in Great Britain at the University Press, Cambridge

British Library cataloguing in publication data
Wetherbee, Winthrop, 1938–
Chaucer: the Canterbury tales. — (Landmarks of world
literature)
1. Poetry in English. Chaucer, Geoffrey, 1340?–1400.
Canterbury tales
I. Title   II. Series
821'.1

Library of Congress cataloging in publication data applied for

ISBN 0 521 32331 2 hard covers
ISBN 0 521 31159 4 paperback

Contents

Chronology

Chaucer's life and works	Literary events	Historical events
		1309 Pope Clement V begins Avignon Papacy
		1327 Edward III (aged 14) crowned
	1335–41 Boccaccio, *Filostrato, Teseida*	
	1337 Birth of Froissart	1337 Edward lays claim to French crown; beginning of Hundred Years' War
1340–45 Birth of Chaucer	1342–43 Petrarch begins *Canzoniere*	
		1343–44 English knights take part in siege of Algeciras (v. *Gen. Prol.* 56–57)
		1346 Victory over French at Crécy; victory over Scots at Neville's Cross
		1348–49 Black Death
	1349–52 Boccaccio, *Decameron*	

1356		Victory over French at Poitiers; John II of France taken captive
1357	In service of Countess of Ulster	
1359–60	Taken prisoner in Normandy; ransomed by Edward III	
1360		Peace of Bretigny leaves Edward in control of one third of France
1361		Black Death reappears
1361–65		Pierre de Lusignan (Peter of Cyprus; v. *Monk's Tale* 2391–98) takes "Satalye" (Adalia), Alexandria, and "Lyeys" (Ayas) (*Gen. Prol.* 51, 57–59)
1367	Granted life annuity by Edward III	
1367		Black Prince defeats mercenary army under Bernard de Guesclin at Najera, Spain, gains throne for Pedro the Cruel (v. *Monk's Tale* 2375–90)
1367–70	Langland, *Piers Plowman*, A Text	
1368	Possible first visit to Italy	

Chaucer's life	Literary events	Historical events
1369–70 *Book of the Duchess*		
1372–73 Visits Genoa and Florence		1371 French reclaim Gascony, Poitiers
	1374 Death of Petrarch	
	1375 Death of Boccaccio	1376 "Good Parliament" condemns waste and profiteering by high government officials
1377 Involved in negotiations toward marriage of Richard to Princess Marie of France		1377 Rye and Hastings burned by French
		1377 Death of Edward III; succeeded by Richard II
1378 Visits Lombardy; appoints John Gower as attorney in his absence		1378 Great Schism in Papacy; Urban VI at Rome (recognized by England); Clement VII at Avignon (recognized by France)
	1380–86 Gower, *Vox Clamantis*	1380s First version of Lollard Bible
		1381 Peasants' Revolt

		1382	Wycliffe's teachings condemned by Blackfriars synod
		138-	Death of Bernabò Visconti of Milan (*Monk's Tale* 2399–406)
1385–87	*Troilus and Crisey*		
1386	Elected to Parliament for Kent		
1387	Begins *Canterbury Tales*		
1388	Annuity transferred to John Scalby, perhaps at instigation of "Merciless Parliament"	1388	"Merciless Parliament"; "Appellants" gain impeachment of officials close to Richard
1389–91	Appointed Clerk of the Works, Commissioner of Walls and Ditches		
1390	Gower, *Confessio Amantis*, dedicated to Richard II		
1393	Gower rededicates *Confessio* to Henry Bolingbroke		
1394	Richard II renews Chaucer's annuity		

	Chaucer's Life		Public Events
1396			Truce with France; England retains only Calais
1397			Parliament undoes work of Merciless Parliament
1398			Banishment of Henry Bolingbroke
1399	Henry IV supplements Chaucer's annuity "for good service"		Deposition of Richard; succeeded by Bolingbroke as Henry IV
1400	Death of Chaucer		

Chapter 1

Introduction

Chaucer and his poem

For most readers the *Canterbury Tales* mean the General Prologue, with its gallery of portraits, and a few of the more humorous tales. What we retain 'is a handful of remarkable personalities, and such memorable moments as the end of the Miller's tale. These are worth having in themselves, but it requires an extra effort to see the significant relationship among them, and to recognize that their bewildering variety is Chaucer's technique for representing a single social reality. We may compare the first part of Shakespeare's *Henry IV*, where our impressions can be so dominated by Falstaff, Hotspur and Hal as to leave Henry and the problems of his reign in shadow. The comparison is the more suggestive in that Shakespeare has recreated the England of Chaucer's last years, when a society that is essentially that of the *Canterbury Tales* was shaken by usurpation, regicide and civil war. Both poets describe a nation unsure of its identity, distrustful of traditional authority, and torn by ambition and materialism into separate spheres of interest. For both, the drives and interactions of individual personalities express a loss of central control, a failure of hierarchy which affects society at all levels.

Shakespeare's focus is always on a single "body politic," and though his characters span all levels of society, their situations are determined by a central crisis of monarchical authority. Chaucer's project is harder to define. He shows us nothing of Shakespeare's royal Westminster, and gives us only a glimpse of his chaotic Eastcheap; and though profoundly political in their implications, the *Tales* offer no comment on contemporary politics. But the Canterbury pilgrims, too, are a society in transition, their horizons enlarged by war and commerce, their relations complicated by new types of enterprise and new social roles. What holds them together is a radically innovative literary structure, a fictional world with no center, defined by oppositions between realistic and idealistic, worldly and religious, traditionalist and individualist points of view.

The center is the teller

The plot of the *Tales* is simple enough. In early April, the narrator is lodged at the Tabard in Southwark, ready to make a pilgrimage to the shrine of St. Thomas à Becket at Canterbury, when a group of twenty-nine pilgrims arrive at the inn. The narrator is admitted to their number and provides portraits of most of the group, each of whom embodies a different aspect of English society. The host of the Tabard, Harry Baily, decides to join the pilgrims, and proposes a game to divert them on the road: all will tell stories, and the best tale will be rewarded at journey's end with a supper at the Tabard. The bulk of the poem consists of the tales of twenty-three pilgrims, interspersed with narrative and dialogue which link their performances to the frame of the pilgrimage journey.

The literary form of the story collection, in which narratives of diverse kinds are organized within a larger framing narrative, had a long history, and had been treated with new sophistication in Chaucer's own time. But neither the *Confessio Amantis* of his friend John Gower, which was in progress during the early stages of his own project, nor Boccaccio's *Decameron*, which he almost certainly knew, exhibits anything like the complexity of the *Tales*. The social diversity of Chaucer's pilgrims, the range of styles they employ, and the psychological richness of their interaction, both with one another and with their own tales, are a landmark in world literature. In no earlier work do characters so diverse in origin and status as Chaucer's "churls" and "gentles" meet and engage on equal terms. In the *Decameron* "churls" exist only as two-dimensional characters in stories told by an aristocratic company. In the *Romance of the Rose*, the thirteenth-century love-allegory which was the greatest single influence on Chaucer's poetry, the low social status

and coarse behavior of "Evil-Tongue" and "Danger" is
allegorical, defining them as threats to the progress of the
poem's courtly lover. But Chaucer's churls exist on the same
plane of reality as the Knight and Prioress. Some are
undeniably beyond the pale in ordinary social terms, and their
membership in the pilgrim company gives them a voice they
could acquire in no other way. Under the rough authority of
the Host, and the wide-eyed, uncritical gaze of the narrator,
characters as mean or unsavory as the Manciple and Summoner take part in a dialogue in which no point of view is
exempt from criticism and conventional social values have
frequently to be laid aside.

The narrator is one of the most remarkable features of the
Tales. He is at once the most innocent and most knowing of
men, seemingly guileless as he points to the revealing traits of
speech and behavior in his fellow pilgrims, yet astute in filling
the gaps created by their reticence, and placing them in relation to the issues affecting their world. Naiveté aside, this narrator must resemble the historical Geoffrey Chaucer, a poet
uniquely qualified by background and experience to produce
a work so broad in its social vision. He was the son of a successful merchant who had served the crown as a customs
official. As an adolescent he entered the service of Elizabeth,
Countess of Ulster and wife of Lionel, Duke of Clarence,
second son of Edward III. Still in his teens, he was captured
while serving with Edward's invading army in France, and
ransomed by the King. From the mid-1360s until his death
around 1400 he served the crown, visiting France and Italy on
diplomatic missions, working as a customs official, sitting on
various commissions and for a term as a Member of Parliament, and acting as Clerk of the Works, in charge of the
maintenance of various royal buildings. He was in close
touch with the worlds of law, commerce, diplomacy, and
warfare, and with the life of the court and aristocracy. He
was also one of the most learned laymen of his day, and one
of the most European in outlook, fully at home with French
culture, and ahead of his time in appreciating the brilliant
achievements of fourteenth-century Italy. And though his

poetry rarely says so directly, he was acutely aware of the grim realities of English politics.

In the last years of Edward III, the heavy taxation required by long and unsuccessful wars, charges of corruption against high officials, and hostility to the wealth and power of the Church were dividing the country. The "Good Parliament" of 1376 indicted several prominent courtiers and financiers, but its attempted reforms had little effect. In the late 1370s a series of poll taxes brought to a head the longstanding grievances of the laboring classes, who, since the labor short-ages caused by the terrible plagues of 1348–49, had seen repeated attempts to control their wages and mobility. In 1381, under the pressures of taxation, anxiety about foreign competition in the cloth trade, and a concern for legal rights, the Peasants' Revolt broke out in several parts of southern England. In London many buildings were burned, including the sumptuous palace of Chaucer's patron John of Gaunt, and a mob killed dozens of Flemish merchants and cloth-workers. Richard II, who had assumed the throne at the age of ten in 1377, showed courage and judgment in negotiating with the rebels, but his later years were marred by favoritism and financial irresponsibility. The Parliament of 1386, in which Chaucer sat as a member for Kent, demanded many reforms, and when Richard refused to accede, battle was joined between the king's supporters and his chief opponents. The rebel lords, who included the future King Henry IV, hav-ing gained a victory at Radcot Bridge in Oxfordshire and marched on London, became the so-called Lords Appellant of the "Merciless Parliament" of 1388, in the course of which a number of Richard's friends and financial backers were sentenced to death.

Chaucer seems to have maintained good relations with the Court through three troubled decades, though his friends in-cluded men deeply involved in the conflicts of the time, some of whom lost their lives. And apart from two disparaging references to the Peasants' Revolt, his poetry never addresses contemporary political issues. He was clearly troubled by the effects of commerce and social mobility: restlessness, ambition, and a concern with power are pervasive among the Pilgrims, and are always suspect. But in matters of practical politics, his view of established authority seems to have been fundamentally conservative.

On religious questions, too, Chaucer is reticent. In a period of mounting hostility to the established Church, he confines his criticism to the specific excesses of the Friar, Pardoner, and Monk. He never addresses the condition of the episcopal hierarchy, or urges any reform more radical than the renewal of fundamental Christian values outlined in the Parson's tale. However, it is likely that he was responsive to evangelical tendencies at work among the lower clergy and laity. Throughout the later fourteenth century the reformers known to their opponents as "Lollards" (mumblers [of prayers]?), inspired by the largely anti-establishment theology of John Wycliffe, sought to free religious practice from the sanctions of the Church hierarchy, and placed a new emphasis on the individual conscience. Though attacked as heretics, their concern to distance religion from worldly institutions had a broad appeal. Chaucer's clear preference for the simple, private piety promoted by the Nun's Priest and the Parson, as against the elaborately self-dramatizing religiosity of the Man of Law and the Prioress, would be fully consonant with Lollard sympathies. We may note that in the "Epilogue" that follows the Man of Law's tale in several manuscripts, the Parson is openly accused of Lollardy, and makes no attempt to deny the charge. The accusation is based on his aversion to the swearing of religious oaths, a typical Lollard attitude with which Chaucer shows sympathy elsewhere. It is possible, too, that the capping of the tale-telling game with the Parson's austere penitential treatise indicates sympathy with the reformers. Certainly Chaucer's friends included the so-called "Lollard Knights," courtiers and men of affairs who gave protection to Lollard preachers and maintained certain distinctive practices and beliefs. The extent of their Lollardy is hard to gauge, but several in their wills requested simple funerals and graves, and asked that money from their estates be given to the poor rather than providing rich funeral feasts or bequests to religious institutions. Such austerity did not prevent their pursuing successful careers as soldiers, diplomats and land-owners, but the contradiction is no greater than that presented by Chaucer's own "Retraction" to the *Canterbury Tales*, in which much of that work and the bulk of his earlier poems are repudiated as "worldly vanitees."

But if Chaucer's position on major questions remains elusive, the form of his poem and its treatment of character are themselves vehicles of serious social criticism. A major project of the *Tales* is the testing of traditional values. In the General Prologue a hierarchical model of society, defined by traditional obligation and privilege, provides a tentative framework, but few of the pilgrims can be said to embody traditional roles in a recognizable form, and theirs are the least palpably real of Chaucer's portraits. More often the rejection or usurpation of traditional roles provides an index to social mobility: again and again such "modern" tendencies as the secularizing of the religious life, or the aspirations of the professions and guilds, take the form of an emulation or appropriation of the style and prerogatives of gentility. Such pretensions are often only a veil for self-interest, but they point up the inadequacy of traditional categories to define the hierarchical position of newly powerful commercial and professional groups concerned to claim a status and dignity of their own. Faced with so many forms of "worthiness," the narrator must finally concede his inability to set his characters "in their degree," the place where they "stand" in traditional social terms.

Chaucer was well situated to appreciate this crisis of values. Familiar as he was with many areas of his society, he was primarily a courtier and a gentleman, for whom courtesy, honor and truth constituted social norms. He would have agreed with the Wife of Bath that gentility bears no inherent relation to birth or fortune, but he clearly saw it as more readily compatible with some ways of life than with others. Hence his portraits of such emergent "gentles" as the Merchant and the Man of Law mix respect for their professional and public functions with a keen awareness of how easily these can coexist with covert or self-deceiving materialism and self-aggrandizement. He would probably have conceded them the status of gentlemen, but there is no clear line between their world and that of the equally professional Shipman and Physician, though the one is perhaps a pirate and the other something of a charlatan.

But if the usurpation of gentility and its prerogatives disturbs Chaucer, the chivalric and courtly ideals are themselves scrutinized in the course of the poem, and it is made clear that they harbor their own inherent contradictions. In keeping with Chaucer's concern for hierarchy, the Knight, highest in rank among the pilgrims, opens the competition with a tale that promotes the virtues of Theseus, conqueror and knightly hero *par excellence*. Unabashedly an argument for chivalry as the basis of social order, the tale nevertheless shows chivalry repeatedly unable to contain or subdue disorder, largely because its only resource is authority imposed from above and reinforced by armed power. Ultimately, the tale is a searching exploration of the limits of the chivalric ethic as a political instrument. Other tales extend this critique to courtly values in general, not only by parody, as in the Miller's rejoinder to the Knight, but by focusing on them directly, as when the Wife of Bath uses the standard of *gentilesse* to expose an Arthurian knight's failure to exhibit true courtly conduct. The Squire's tale, the imaginative vision of a knight in embryo, shows naiveté and confusion coexisting with real virtues in a young mind that takes courtly values wholly for granted. And the Franklin, a man (like Chaucer) at home on the border between the courtly and practical worlds, subjects the ethical contradictions of the courtly code to a peculiarly modern scrutiny, showing that much of what seems foolish in the Squire's performance is inherent in the courtly ideal itself.

And of course the world of the *Tales* includes a number of characters who are not courtly, for whom the narrator feels a need to apologize and whose coarseness he carefully disowns. The importance of the opposition of "churls" to "gentles" is established by the opening cluster of tales, in which the Knight's cumbersome celebration of order is challenged by the brilliant and broadly salutary parody of the Miller, and this in turn by the largely *ad hominem* thrust of the Reeve. The descent from highly serious poetry to parody to personal attack implies a breakdown of social order that ends in the flight of the Cook's wayward apprentice; as the Cook's narrative disintegrates into the random particulars of London lowlife, we are left at an immense distance from the ceremonial world of Theseus. The social oppositions defined in this opening sequence do not appear again in so clear-cut a form, but their implications pervade the entire poem.

The tension between large, public concerns like those of the Knight and the narrower vision of the churls is also expressed in a contrast of literary genres. Like the Knight, the gentle Squire and Franklin tell tales that can be defined as *romance*, centered on the world of chivalry and courtly idealism. The typical mode of the churls, brilliantly exemplified by the Miller's and Reeve's tales, is the *fabliau*, a short comic tale, often deliberately coarse, which normally deals with a bourgeois or lower-class world and emphasizes action, cleverness, and the gratification of instinct. This opposition of genres, too, is clearest in the opening sequence; in later tales romance and fabliau elements are often combined with one another, or adapted to other concerns. In the Merchant's history of the marriage of January a grotesque attempt at romance is gradually transformed into the fabliau of the elderly hero's betrayal. The Wife of Bath describes her own marital history in terms that are very much those of the world of fabliau, but then, through her intense imagining of a life in which women would be valued at their true worth and treated with real *gentilesse*, she transcends that world. From the rough-and-tumble of her fifth marriage she emerges into an equilibrium of mutual respect, and the passage from her prologue to her tale is simultaneously a passage from fabliau to romance. Romance becomes self-critical in the hands of the Franklin, and fabliau is a vehicle for satire in the Summoner's rejoinder to the Friar. And the tale of the Shipman, who dwells on the border between the world of the professionals and that of the churls, is in effect an upper-class fabliau, pragmatic and mechanical in treating economic and sexual motivation, but deceptively subtle in presenting the private world of its merchant protagonist.

There is a broad pattern in the interaction of romance and fabliau in the *Tales*, an increasing tendency to expose the contradictions and absurdities of the one accompanied by a perceptible rise in the dignity of the other. The shift expresses an increasingly pragmatic approach to the social reality the poem engages, an uneasiness with traditional categories and a desire to bring emerging social forces into confrontation. A broadly similar opposition can be observed among the tales of religion. The first of these, the Man of Law's tale, presents itself as a religious counterpart to the Knight's, comparable in solemnity and historical perspective, and similarly committed to affirming order in the face of the uncertainties of earthly life. The Man of Law's Custance is an emperor's daughter and the "mirror of all courtesy," and her story has been aptly described as "hagiographic romance." The rich rhetoric of prayer and sentiment in the Prioress's tale is similarly indebted to courtly poetry. At the opposite pole are the Nun's Priest's Aesopian fable of the cock and the fox and the spare penitential treatise of the Parson. Together they present a daunting challenge to religious emotionalism and high style, as the blunt colloquialism and materialist skepticism of the churls debunk the ideals of romance.

But the tales of Man of Law and Prioress, whatever their effect as vehicles of religious sentiment, also express distinctive points of view toward the world. The Man of Law's horror of the familial tensions that continually threaten his Custance, and the broader anxiety about earthly justice that pervades his tale, at times getting the better of his faith in Providence, are the preoccupations of a man who knows these problems at first hand. The Prioress's tale is marred by a violence and anti-Semitism that are no less horrible for being virtually invisible to the Prioress herself, and expose the emotional privation behind her façade of genteel and complacent piety. The social and spiritual complexities revealed in

the process of tale-telling are the real focus of both performances, and remind us of the importance of character as
a vehicle of social criticism, the extent to which we must rely
on the often distorted vision of the pilgrims themselves to
gauge the bearing of great issues on their lives.

Chaucer goes to extraordinary lengths to show the
obstacles to vision and knowledge posed by the pilgrims'
existential situations, and we may compare his perspective to
that of the great Franciscan philosopher of the previous
generation, William of Ockham. "Ockham's razor" is often
said to have severed philosophy from theology: this is an
exaggeration, but his denial of the necessity of natural secondary causes (since there is nothing God might effect through
a secondary cause that He is not equally able to accomplish
directly), and his confinement of *scientia*, or real knowledge,
to the sphere of observation and logical inference, tend in this
direction. They allow us to affirm little about the relation of
created life to God beyond the acknowledgment, through
faith, of his omnipotence and goodness, and the ethical
imperative of obeying his commands. Chaucer accepts similar
constraints for his characters. Theseus' evocation of the
benevolent "First Mover," insofar as it is more than a
political gesture, is a leap of faith, and a pervasive concern of
the *Tales* as a whole is the psychological effect of living with
no more immediate confirmation of order and providence
than such a leap provides. Some characters simply refuse to
consider "Who hath the world in honde"; others reveal their
anxiety in such neurotic forms as the Man of Law's vacillating attitude toward Providence or the Pardoner's compulsive blasphemy; and the Nun's Priest, apparently after
serious thought, seems to have made peace with the likelihood
that the large questions of providence and self-determination
are unanswerable.

Cut off from a sure sense of relation to the divine, or of
their place in a traditional hierarchy, the pilgrims question
their own status. Many of the tales are essays in self-
definition, attempts to establish values and goals that lead to
startling revelations. The Knight, whose tale begins as an

apology for chivalry, finds himself unable to bring it to a satisfying resolution, and is carried steadily toward a confrontation with the horror of violence and death which challenges his chivalric values. The Wife of Bath, trying to justify a life of striving for mastery in marriage, becomes half-aware that her deepest need is to be recognized and valued as a woman, something of which her society seems incapable. The Pardoner flaunts his success as a religious huckster and defies the taboo effect of his sexual abnormality, but gradually reveals a religious inner self that accepts the paradoxical guilt of the scapegoat, an agonizing display that illustrates the intolerance of a Christian society. In all these cases the tale-tellers' struggles are rendered more painful by a vision of order or harmony or forgiveness that seems to hover just out of reach.

The elaborate context in which Chaucer's characters live and think is again a landmark in literary history. To compare the Wife of Bath or the Pardoner with the embodiments of lechery and hypocrisy in the *Romance of the Rose* on whom they are modeled is to see at once the greater depth and complexity of Chaucer's creations. The noble company who tell the tales of the *Decameron* are social equals with no personal history, charming but limited by their very urbanity. Their relations with one another and with the tales they tell exhibit none of the interplay that gives the *Canterbury Tales* their rich complexity. The closest equivalent to the dense social and psychological medium in which Chaucer's characters function is the *Inferno* of Dante, and their self-revelations are often as powerful as those of Dante's sinners. But Dante's characters are necessarily static, fixed forever in the attitudes defined by their besetting sins; Chaucer's are alive, able to exercise their imaginations in ways which unexpectedly open up new dimensions in their lives. Their condition is one of radical uncertainty and vast possibility.

The project of tale-telling is of course what keeps the lives of the pilgrims open-ended, and the juxtaposition and interaction of the tales are the basis of the poem's structure. To address the difficult question of the pattern that emerges as the sequence of tales runs its course, we may divide the poem into a series of broad movements. The first is bracketed by the tales of the Knight and the Man of Law, the two major attempts in the poem to address the problem of order. The Knight's tale, as I have suggested, is undone by contradictions inherent in the chivalric code. In the Man of Law's tale commitment is undermined by personal anxiety. He loudly affirms God's abiding concern for Custance, but feels a need to supplement Providence with an officiousness of his own which ensures that her contact with the world is minimal. Custance never becomes real, her human constancy is never tried, and the narrator remains torn between commitment to faith in God and an irrepressible fear of imminent danger. Thus this first group of tales calls into question the authoritarian models proposed by the two highest-ranking pilgrims. The challenge to order which surfaces in the Knight's tale and is elaborated in the descending movement of the tales that follow, as social vision is increasingly narrowed by personal concerns, is recapitulated in the Man of Law's tale as a conflict in the narrator's own view of the world.

In the broad central area of the poem, social criticism is on a smaller scale. The problem of authority in marriage, introduced in spectacular fashion by the Wife of Bath, is a recurring theme, punctuated by the naming of the Wife in the tales of both Clerk and Merchant, and climaxed by the Franklin's exhaustive catalogue of the things that make for success in marriage. The astute perceptions of the Shipman likewise center on domestic relations. Otherwise the tales of this section are largely fueled by private concerns. The social conflict dramatized in the first fragment reappear on a reduced scale in the mutual hostility of Friar and Summoner, which combines criticism of institutions with *ad hominem* malevolence, and the closest equivalents to the institutional commitments of the Knight and Man of Law are the Squire's breathless and abortive flight of courtly idealism and the tormented piety of the Prioress's miracle story. The tales of Merchant and Physician are circumscribed by the materialism of their tellers, and the Wife and Pardoner are concerned as much with their status as human beings as with the issues implied by their social roles.

In the midst of the varied company of this central group, the Clerk's tale stands out with stark clarity. The story of patient Griselde and her tyrannical husband has been explained as answering the Wife of Bath's challenge to male authority in marriage by vindicating the traditional, misogynistically conceived institution as a proving-ground of virtue. But in the end, as the intensity of Griselde's suffering forces its way to the surface, what we learn is that the constraints imposed on her are indeed "importable" (unbearable). The Clerk's story is a searching comment on power and authority, not only in the social context implied by the role of Walter, an Italian minor tyrant of a kind Chaucer may have observed at first hand, but in the institutionalizing of moral values and the creation of moral fiction. The almost perversely beautiful style which sets off the prolonged sufferings of Griselde cannot wholly conceal a substructure of sado-masochistic fantasy. The appropriation of her femininity to an ostensibly moral and spiritual purpose is at times perilously close to the fetishistic treatment of emblematic figures in other tales. This tendency is present in the Man of Law's overprotection of Custance, and is carried to extremes in the cases of the twelve-year-old Virginia of the Physician's tale or the Prioress's child-martyr. The Clerk's tale has superficial affinities with these tales of sainthood, but its purpose is humane rather than hagiographical. The convoluted irony of his performance is finally unfathomable, but a number of features of his tale hint at an underlying sympathy with the Wife's attempt to redefine sexual relations, and it is perhaps the most fully achieved of all the tales in its rendering of the complexities it addresses.

The four tales which follow are concerned with the value of fiction itself, and the project of the *Canterbury Tales* in particular. The pilgrim narrator's paired tales, *Sir Thopas* and *Melibee*, present a polar opposition of form and style. *Sir Thopas*, a comic romance rendered almost chaotic by a proliferation of incident and the confusion of its hero's motives, reflects the array of problems Chaucer has set himself in the *Tales* as a whole by his deliberate indulgence of the eccentric energies of his pilgrims. In the *Melibee*, a moral argument is expounded with virtually no regard for narrative or personality, and the result is a cumbersome tale whose human significance never emerges. The opposition between the brilliant parody of the one tale and the ponderous moral eloquence of the other show Chaucer aware of the difficulty of synthesizing his brilliant and varied gifts and adapting them to the presentation of a coherent world view.

The tales of the Monk and the Nun's Priest form a similar pairing, one that invites us to ponder the relevance of epic and tragedy to the concrete and often homely world of the *Tales*. The Monk's collection of nineteen stories of the falls of great men represents a form Chaucer's own collection might have taken, a group of exemplary stories organized by a common concern with the workings of fortune. But like the *Melibee*, the Monk's tale attains coherence only at the price of fragmenting history and falsifying character to reduce its material to simple moral terms. The contrasting tale of the Nun's Priest is the Aesopian fable of the cock and the fox, lavishly embellished with epic and tragic rhetoric, vivid stories illustrating the truth and value of dreams, and speculation on the theological meaning of Chauntecleer's capture by the fox. The implicit suggestion that such materials, the resources of some of Chaucer's most serious poetry, are as applicable to the story of a rooster as to human affairs poses in a new way the question of how literature engages reality.

A third pairing, between the tales of the Second Nun and the Canon's Yeoman, develops the spiritual implications of Chaucer's concern with the problems of tale-telling, and points forward toward the religious emphasis of the poem's conclusion. There is a precise thematic contrast between the Yeoman's largely confessional tale of the desperate, failed, and finally specious project of "translation" undertaken by his alchemists, and the Second Nun's impersonal and authoritative depiction of the religious transformations wrought by St. Cecilia. The alchemists' murky world of fumes, toil, and blind obsession is the antithesis of the tranquil assurance and radiant spirituality with which Cecilia and her companions are vested. The balancing of these tales defines the absolute limits of human art, and the necessity of spiritual authority as a supplement to earthly vision. The two tales that conclude the poem reinforce this point in a way that directly implicates the project of the *Canterbury Tales*. Both are dismissive of fiction, but their messages are sharply opposed. The Manciple's anti-moral − that it is better not to speak than to risk the consequences of doing so − seems to deny and mock the very idea of serious fiction, and the Parson's total rejection of "fable" presents the same lesson in a positive form. For the expected verse tale he substitutes a treatise in prose, designed to aid penitents in considering the state of their souls, and including a detailed analysis of the deadly sins and their remedies. As the last of the tales, the Parson's treatise is a part of the larger economy of the poem. But its effect is to withdraw us to another plane of reality, enabling us to see the world of the previous tales in perspective, and encouraging us to turn our minds to higher things.

Before we proceed to look more closely at the poem itself, something must be said about its probable contemporary audience. No poem lends itself better to oral presentation, and we can be sure that it was read aloud, but it shows none of the conventional signs of address to a mixed audience of courtly aristocrats that mark Chaucer's earlier poetry. The *Canterbury Tales* are a boldly experimental work, and it is probable that the audience to whom Chaucer looked for a fully appreciative reception were those most involved in the changes affecting the world the poem describes. In a verse *envoy* (letter) to his friend Bukton, Chaucer urges him to "rede" the Wife of Bath before entering into marriage; the word can bear several meanings, but it is probable that what is being suggested is a private rereading of the Wife's Prologue, and probable too that the poem as a whole was aimed most directly at readers capable of thoughtful engagement with the issues raised by Chaucer's poetry. Though a new insight into the condition of women is one of the chief rewards the poem offers, its audience was no doubt largely male. Whether knights, civil servants or men of learning, law, or commerce, they are likely to have been gentlemen who, like Chaucer himself, had learned to function in several worlds, and had few illusions about the workings of justice, commerce, or aristocratic and ecclesiastical power. Such men would recognize clearly the difference between "churl" and "gentle," and the Peasants' Revolt may have sharpened their sense of it; but in an age of social mobility they would also recognize that such distinctions were not absolute, and in some cases might even have been drawn by Lollard sympathies into a closer sense of relation to those of lower station. We may assume that the *Canterbury Tales* did for them what they can still do for us, making them more aware and more tolerant of human diversity, and so, in a sense of the word important to Chaucer, more gentle.

Chaucer's language

Chaucer spoke and wrote the English of the South East Midland region, the language of Gower and Wycliffe, the spoken language of London, and the branch of Middle English from which our own English most directly descends. By Chaucer's day English was rapidly recovering from its displacement by French as the language of the upper and administrative classes. Legal and other public documents began to be produced in English, translation from French and Latin was steadily increasing, and there is evidence of English replacing French in grammar schools.

The language was not the essentially synthetic language that Old English had been. During the long dominance of French, and partly under its influence, the inflections that had indicated the number and case of nouns had largely disappeared in favor of a greater reliance on prepositions, and those indicating the tense and person of verbs were being replaced by auxiliary verbs. The native processes of coinage, the combining of existing words or the addition of prefixes and suffixes to form new compounds, had largely fallen into disuse because of the ready availability of equivalent French terms. The result of these developments is a language much closer to our own than Old English, but we must still allow for many peculiarities: elliptical or paratactic syntax; double and triple negatives; the omission of articles; the habit of forming the negative of such verbs as *witen* (know), *wile* (will or wish) and *ben* (be) by replacing the initial consonant, if any, with *n*.

But for most students the chief obstacle to reading Chaucer in his own language is the unfamiliar look of Middle English spelling, in which *y* often replaces *i*, and a word can appear in several different forms in a single text. This is in part the inconsistency of an orthography which was not to be standardized for another 300 years, but it also reflects the fluid state of pronunciation and accent. At a time when English was drawing freely on French for its vocabulary, the patterns of stress proper to the two languages seem to have been to some extent interchangeable, and Chaucer exploits this circumstance to achieve some of his most striking metrical effects. In polysyllabic words of French or Latin origin such as "daungerous," "adversitee," or "memorie," the main stress may fall on the final syllable, as we hear it in French, or occur earlier, as in modern English. At times the same freedom is exercised with non-French words. "Sórrow" appears also as "sorówe," and as the vestigially Anglo-Saxon monosyllable "sorwe." Terminal *e*, originally a grammatical inflection, had become largely a convenience in pronunciation, and Chaucer frequently relies on it to sustain the iambic movement of a line, though it also occurs at points where the meter requires that it be suppressed.

Hearing Chaucer's English can do a great deal for comprehension, and there are a few basic rules. Middle English vowels sound approximately as in a modern European language: short *a* has the sound of modern German "Mann" rather than modern English "hat"; short *o* is closer to "long" than to American "got"; short *u* is as in "put" rather than "putt." Of the diphthongs, *au* has the sound of *ou* in modern "loud," and *ou* that of *oo* in modern "food." All consonants are pronounced, so that in a word like "knight," monosyllabic for metrical purposes, the "k" and "gh" (= *ch* in modern German *ich*) are clearly audible.

In general, for speakers of modern English, and especially for those used to American English, Middle English at first requires a certain physical effort to pronounce, but soon becomes a physical pleasure. It is helpful to begin by exaggerating each sound, and noting the role of teeth, tongue, palate, and lips in producing it. A mirror and a tape recorder can be very useful, and I have listed some recordings of portions of the *Canterbury Tales* in the bibliography.

The text of the *Canterbury Tales*

The *Canterbury Tales* are incomplete. What survives is a series of fragments, usually consisting of two or more tales whose sequence is clear. In general there is good manuscript evidence for the ordering of these fragments, and scholars now accept almost unanimously the order of the handsome early fifteenth-century Ellesmere Manuscript. Like nearly all manuscripts, Ellesmere reflects some scribal editing. It frequently regularizes meter and even syntax, sometimes obscuring Chaucer's meaning in the process. In this respect it is inferior to the Hengwrt manuscript, evidently produced by the same scribe and much less heavily edited. But the links and juxtapositions of tales in Ellesmere are far more plausible than in Hengwrt (which, among other peculiarities, omits the Canon's Yeoman's tale altogether). It seems likely that Ellesmere reflects a later and more leisurely editorial process, and it provides the basis for most standard editions.

The ten fragments of the text in Ellesmere are arranged as follows:

I.   General Prologue, Knight, Miller, Reeve, Cook
II.   Man of Law
III. Wife of Bath, Friar, Summoner
IV.   Clerk, Merchant
V.   Squire, Franklin
VI.   Physician, Pardoner

VII.   Shipman, Prioress, *Sir Thopas*, *Melibee*, Monk, Nun's Priest
VIII. Second Nun, Canon's Yeoman
IX.   Manciple
X.   Parson, Chaucer's Retraction

In what follows I have taken the Ellesmere ordering for granted, though I have indicated places where my reasons for doing so were chiefly thematic. All quotations are from the *Riverside Chaucer*, ed. Larry D. Benson (Boston, 1987). Roman numerals indicate Ellesmere fragments.

Chapter 2

The General Prologue

In a time when French poetry was still the dominant influence on aristocratic taste in England, Chaucer's literary range was unusually broad. Fully at home with the French tradition, he was widely read in Latin poetry and philosophy, classical and medieval, and he was perhaps the first non-Italian to fully appreciate the achievement of Dante, Petrarch, and Boccaccio. One result of this extensive literary culture is a remarkably rich poetic vocabulary. Chaucer fundamentally altered the expressive capacities of English by drawing much of his language from these sources, and he moves among them with brilliant effect, balancing the colloquial force of English with coinages from the learned Latin tradition and the courtly vernaculars of France and Italy.

Middle English was peculiarly well suited to such linguistic play. The Norman Conquest had imposed on England a French-speaking aristocracy and administrative hierarchy, relegating the native vernacular to a largely sub-literate status. English had been reasserting itself since the early thirteenth century, but showed the effect of "colonization" in a tendency to accord a higher status to words drawn from French than to their English equivalents. Later, as the language of learning and formal devotion was adapted to English, Latinate terms became similarly privileged. Evidence of the relative status of the three languages pervades Chaucer's poetry. In the Reeve's tale the essence of the social ambition of the miller Symkyn is distilled in the rich French rhyme that expresses his anger at the presumption of the clerk Aleyn to "disparáge" his daughter and her "lynáge" (birth). The Pardoner, discovering matter for a sermon in the human digestive processes, gives weight to his invective by pairing the simple English "dung" with the

Latinate, abstract and morally connotative "corruption."
Elsewhere the interplay of Latin, Romance, and English is
less hierarchical and more complex. In *Troilus and Criseyde*,
love is invoked in these lines:

> Plesance of love, O goodly debonaire,[1]   [1] gracious
> In gentil hertes ay[1] redy to repaire[2]   [1] ever [2] dwell
> O veray[1] cause of heele[2] and of gladnesse,   [1] true [2] health
> Iheryed[1] be thy myght and thi goodnesse!   [1] praised

In the first couplet courtly love, proper as if by nature to
those of gentle breeding, is aptly described in the diction of
Romance lyric (the second line echoes a famous *canzone* of
the Italian poet Guido Guinizelli). In line three, "veray
cause" is both good French and good Latin (*vera causa*), hinting at a more authoritative, religious or philosophical concept
of love. In the fourth line invocation becomes explicitly
prayer, authority emerges as power, and the new directness is
set off by language as primordially English as Caedmon's
Hymn. The linguistic shifts express the thematic complexity
of the *Troilus*, where the courtly view of love as beautiful and
benign coexists with an intermittent awareness of its irresist-
ible power, in which "myght" is often more apparent than
goodness.

But the finest example in all Chaucer's poetry of the
deployment of contrasting types of language is the opening of
the *Canterbury Tales*:

> Whan that Aprill with his shoures[1] soote[2]   [1] showers [2] sweet
> The droghte[1] of March hath perced to the
>   roote,   [1] drought
> And bathed every veyne in swich[1] licour   [1] such
> Of which vertu engendred is the flour;
> Whan Zephirus eek[1] with his sweete breeth   [1] also
> Inspired hath in every holt and heeth
> The tendre croppes, and the yonge sonne
> Hath in the Ram his halve cours yronne,[1]   [1] run
> And smale foweles[1] maken melodye,   [1] birds
> That slepen al the nyght with open ye[1]   [1] eye
> (So priketh hem nature in hir[1] corages);[2]   [1] their [2] ardor
> Thanne longen folk to goon[1] on pilgrimages.   [1] go

The twelve lines exhibit a variety of diction: personifications proper to Latin poetry ("Aprill," "Zephirus," the "yonge sonne," the signs of the zodiac); terms suggesting an analytical, quasi-scientific perception of the processes at work ("droghte," "veyne," "licour," "engendred"); and the simple English words for natural phenomena ("roote," "holt and heeth," "croppes"). Certain words are referable to several categories. "Vertu," for example, has a range of moral and aesthetic associations in courtly poetry, and as the Latin *virtus* it denotes a force or quality, natural or spiritual. The interrelation of different terms is as important as their evocative range. In the first four lines, an interplay of abstract and concrete ("Aprill" versus "shoures," "droghte" versus "roote") is accentuated by a difficult transition ("swich licour / Of which vertu"): spring rain is identified with an undefined power that descends into the world to effect a kind of incarnation, translating its informing "vertu" into the "flour" of new life.

In the lines that follow, the same process is described in human and sexual terms. "Zephirus," like "Aprill" in the opening line, is a quasi-divinity who "inspires" natural growth. Before Chaucer this English verb had almost invariably signified religious inspiration, but here it is a literal in-breathing: "sweete breeth," a conventional mark of courtliness, suggests a spirit that moves over the landscape like a refined and gentle lover, while the association of the "yonge" sun with Aries implies a sexual energy that becomes explicit in the lines that follow. The restlessness of mating birds is glossed by a still more elaborate linguistic interplay: "So priketh hem nature in hir corages." "Nature," the system of cause and effect that sustains the physical universe, is also personified as a goddess in a range of philosophical poetry, Latin and French. The "corage" in which the sexual impulses of the birds arise is a distinctly human attribute. In addition to its general reference to active feeling, it has associations in courtly poetry which, when recalled in this context, endow the birds' mating impulse with gently comic overtones of chivalric aspiration and derring-do. The incongruity is sustained as nature's authority is conveyed to the "corage" of her creatures, not by semi-divine "inspiration" or cosmic "engendrure," but by "pricking," a verb whose phallic immediacy stresses the elemental character of the feeling evoked.

The long, effortlessly flowing series of parallel clauses ("Whan . . . Whan . . . Thanne . . .") traces a cosmic renewal which descends by stages from the semi-mystical to the crudely physical: all of this, it is implied, is the work of divine *vertu*. Thus when the long sentence arrives at last at its main clause and the poem begins to move forward, the whole complex of cosmic forces informs the impulse to pilgrimage and endows it with a similar complexity. Due tribute is paid to the beneficent influence of the martyr enshrined at Canterbury, but as the Prologue unfolds we hear almost nothing more on this theme, and the motivation of the several pilgrims comes to seem as diverse as their social stations.

The *Canterbury Tales* constitute in certain respects a fundamental break with Chaucer's earlier poetry, which had been centered in the courtly tradition and concerned largely with the implications of the courtly view of human love. Chaucer never wholly abandoned the courtly ideal, and a major concern in the *Tales* is to explore the relation of its values to a changing world. But from the outset its role is strictly qualified. The introductory references to springtime and birdsong, perhaps the oldest and most widespread convention of medieval courtly poetry, show Chaucer placing himself in the tradition of Guillaume de Lorris, author of the love-vision which was the original form of the *Romance of the Rose*. But as Guillaume's delicate allegory was transformed by the continuator of the *Romance*, Jean de Meun, into a narrative of worldly intrigue and seduction, so here the decorum of the love-vision no sooner begins to operate than it is disrupted, as Chaucer's rhythms and diction begin to express an increasingly palpable desire. Rather than introducing a courtly idyll or spiritual quest, this movement propels the pilgrimage forward into direct engagement with the concrete fourteenth-century world.

As the General Prologue proceeds, the rhythm of "descent" continues to operate in various ways. We descend from the initial portrait of the Knight, highest in rank of the pilgrims, to end with figures whose relation to the social order is marginal and predatory. The pilgrims submit to the unofficial authority of Harry Baily, and the spiritual orientation of pilgrimage is replaced by a competition in tale-telling. But the descent is not a continuous movement. As the pilgrims are introduced in succession, their descriptions involve the same interplays of abstract and concrete, the same suggestions and disruptions of hierarchy already apparent in the opening lines. Individual portraits range from ideal types, confections of attributes and values with no individuality, to representations couched wholly in particulars of dress, physical appearance, or behavior. Along this spectrum Chaucer associates each pilgrim with a recognizable social role, and invites us to consider how the subject fulfills our expectations for that role. By these means, and while keeping explicit commentary to a bare minimum, the poet and his narrator explore the shifting relationship between the traditional social hierarchy and a random array of occupations whose purposes and standards are more or less self-determined.

As Jill Mann has shown, many of the pilgrim portraits are based on a long tradition of social satire, and details of dress and behavior allude to the vices conventionally associated with particular occupations. But the narrator never pronounces the moral judgment these telling details imply. He disconcertingly hints at sympathy for characters whom traditional satire would be bound to condemn, and the net effect of his portraits is often puzzlingly at odds with the apparent import of their conventional material. He tends to play to the pilgrims' strengths, or what they consider to be their strengths, sometimes idealizing them to the point at which they become unreal, sometimes rendering a character so nearly in his own words as to make him effectively condemn himself, while giving no explicit sign that he is anything but a "good fellow." In sum, the narrator's perspective on his characters can vary as widely as his applications of epithets

like "worthy" and "gentil," and we can no more discover a
consistent moral or satirical design than explain why a
character like the Shipman or Manciple or Miller should have
taken it into his head to undertake a pilgrimage. When we try
to extract a clear judgment from a portrait, we usually find
ourselves in the uneasy position of having to assume that the
narrator's words mean something other than what they say, or
basing our interpretation on what is not said rather than what
is.

The problem is plain in the opening portrait of the **Knight**.
Ostensibly a paragon of Christian chivalry, he has also been
viewed as a cold-blooded professional whose involvement in
some of the most brutal fighting of his day is in glaring contrast to his perfect courtesy and honor. The structure of the
portrait sets off the contrast. Two passages describing the
Knight's chivalry, which if joined together would comprise an
unambiguously ideal portrait, are separated by a long list of
the Knight's campaigns, fought at various points along the
Christian frontier extending from Spain through North
Africa and Asia Minor to Russia and the Baltic. Many of the
Knight's battles have had a religious purpose, and this,
together with the ascetic cast of his description, suggests the
vocation of the Crusader. But he has fought at least once in
the service of one "heathen" ruler against another, and this,
while it does not clearly imply his reduction to mercenary
status, at least suggests a centrifugal tendency, the possibility
that his sense of purpose has become blurred over the course
of his long sojourn in distant lands. The "lord" in whose
wars he has proven "full worthy" is increasingly difficult to
identify.

There is probably no way either to reconcile these inter-
pretations or to choose between them, yet the sum of the
Knight's campaigns is all the life he is given. Chaucer assigns
him no social or political role in England, and says nothing
of the traditional knightly obligation to keep the peace and
defend the weak. This absence can be taken neither as a sign
of neglect of duty nor as evidence that the Knight is wholly
an embodiment of the crusading ideal. But in the context of

the General Prologue, where English society is the central concern, it invites us to question the status of the Knight and his values in this place and time, and this question should be in our minds as we proceed to the Knight's tale.

The **Squire**'s and **Yeoman**'s portraits, which follow in due hierarchy on to that of the Knight, provide little purchase for the seeker of irony. The **Squire**, too, is a personified abstraction, an embodiment of courtliness and the accomplishments proper to it, rather than chivalry, though he too has served in the field and is clearly a knight in the making. He has no more individuality than the flowering meadow and songbirds to which he is compared, but his conventional attributes, unlike the Knight's, are represented in terms of appearance, and such concrete acts as that of carving for his father. The **Yeoman** is still more concrete, defined by the trappings of his two functions as foot-soldier and forester. His long-bow recalls the role played by this weapon in the wars of Edward III, and so, like the naming of lands where the Knight and Squire have campaigned, places him in recent history, but he too remains essentially a timeless figure. Thus the perceptible shift from abstract to concrete in the detail of the successive portraits does not bring us any closer to social realities. The three pilgrims form a clear hierarchy, but while they thus remind us of traditional social theory, they also hint at the obsolescence of the ideal that theory expresses, and they are relegated together to a position on the margin of the social world of the Prologue.

In contrast, the three representatives of religion whose portraits follow are very much products of their situation in contemporary society, affluent, sexual, class-conscious beings whose relation to the world is dynamic. Secular and courtly rather than religious models provide the most obvious standard of comparison for all three. The **Prioress** is first and foremost a woman seeking to appear genteel. We learn of her religious role only after we have first observed her demure smile, the mildness of her oaths, her manner of singing, the "fair" though provincial character of her French, and finally, at some length, her table manners. None of the "courtly"

traits enumerated is appropriate to a nun, but the point is less
to censure her affectations than to set off the guileless effort
that goes into them. The ensuing account of her more
spiritual side is confined to her tender expressions of sympathy at the sufferings of little animals, suggesting a shallow-
ness to be lightly mocked but not condemned. The concluding
lines note her grey eyes, small nose, and full figure, and the
becomingness of her habit and rosary, but again manage to
suggest an awkwardness in the attempt of her femininity to
resist the constraints of her vocation. The violence and
hostility of her tale will give us a different perspective on the
unconscious power of her feminine nature, but the portrait
shows us a woman who believes in her pretensions, and probably considers herself a successful synthesis of sophistication
and piety.

The **Monk** displays a more challenging worldliness. In his
sumptuous dress and his devotion to hunting he is a male
counterpart to the Prioress, and there is an obvious comple-
mentarity between the Prioress's brooch, with its ambiguous
inscription *Amor vincit omnia* (Love conquers all things),
and the "love-knot" that fastens the Monk's hood. But while
the Prioress's femininity is asserted only in details of manner
and adornment, the Monk is emphatically "a manly man,"
and there is a strong sexual overtone in the references to his
"venerie" (hunting) and "prikyng" (riding, tracking). His
aristocratic style is more fully assimilated than the Prioress's,
and in his deliberate rejection of the cloister he seems to have
lost all understanding of the traditional emphases of monastic
culture. He is nowhere more "manly" than in the vigor with
which his own voice informs the narrator's reporting of his
scorn for the monastic life:

> What[1] sholde he studie and make hymselven
> wood,[2]   [1] why [2] mad
> Upon a book in cloystre alwey to poure,
> Or swynken[1] with his handes, and laboure,   [1] work
> As Austyn[1] bit?[2] How shal the world be   [1] Augustine
> served?   [2] bade
> Lat Austyn have his swynk[1] to hym
> reserved!   [1] work
> (I.184–88)

Product of the modern world that he is, the Monk bears a through-the-looking-glass resemblance to the soldier hierarchy, blending the physical presence of the Yeoman with the pursuits and rich appurtenances of knighthood on its home ground. While the Knight has labored on the fringes of the Christian world, the Monk through his "outriding" as an overseer of monastic lands has established himself in a quasi-knightly role at home. His "courtliness" is a matter of style and avocation, but he brings us close to what knightly behavior in its domestic aspect must have been like in a way that the "perfect" Knight cannot.

The **Friar**'s milieu is that of the tavern and the countryside, but he is clearly paired with the Squire, and his repertory of skills parodies the Squire's grace and versatility. Both are courteous and "lowly of service," though the Friar is so selectively, and with an eye to profit. As confessor, musician, wrestler and bon-vivant, skillful in speech and dalliance, he is all things to all men and women, and his adaptability appears in the shifty language of his description, where "wanton" and "merry" give way abruptly to "solemn," the Latinate sonority of "confessioun" and "absolucioun" is interspersed with homely reminders of his "sweet" and "easy" manner, "honesty" is the cultivation of the rich, and "virtue" denotes skill in begging. His versatility, moreover, is sanctioned, as the frequent references to his "order" suggest. The Prioress's worldliness is largely innocent, and the Monk's is a matter of personal self-assertion, but the Friar, though his life is utterly at odds with the fraternal ideal of holy poverty, seems to speak and act for his order in all that he does.

The four portraits that follow comprise what may be called the minor gentry. Merchant, Clerk and Man of Law are professional men, their status wholly defined by their occupations, but all three might be the landless younger sons of families like the Franklin's. A certain concern for the common weal links them to the traditional gentry: in the Clerk's offering of prayer and instruction in return for his scholar's freedom, or in the unstinting hospitality of the Franklin, we see vestiges of a remembered, or wistfully imagined, social order, in which an exchange of services was the defining principle. Yet the status of all four "gentles" is problematical: none can be said to deviate from a clearly defined norm, as the regular clergy have strayed from their vocations, but their roles are hard to correlate with any clear system of values, and in the case of Merchant or Lawyer, inseparable from the cultivation of private interest. They thus mark a transition from the system of traditional roles and prerogatives to a new, self-defining world of middle-class enterprise and self-assertion.

The **Merchant** has something like the anonymous reserve and dignity of the Knight, and his relation to the world of the lower gentry and middle class corresponds to the Knight's place as the first of the traditional types. Like the Knight, he is repeatedly called "worthy," and characterized largely in terms of prudence and responsibility. But while the Knight is the duly constituted guardian of Christendom itself, the Merchant's only concern is to maintain the routes through which his goods travel between England and the continent; his campaigns are limited to the manipulation of "shields" (coins) on the foreign currency market. Everything about him is self-protective and ambiguous: whereas we need only to be told of the Knight that "he was not gay" to believe implicitly in his gravity and dignity, the Merchant's carefully maintained façade provokes questions rather than forestalling them. The narrator ends by noting that he did not learn his name, and his assertions of his worth and "winning" (profit) hint that he may actually be in debt. The Knight's values remain unquestioned, however precarious their standing in the modern world, whereas the Merchant's assertion of dignity does not express any values at all.

The austere and morally sententious **Clerk** seems to point up by contrast the acquisitiveness and empty self-assertion of the Merchant. Lean and threadbare, offering his prayers as a return for the donations that enable him to pursue his studies, he belongs as wholly to the world of scholarship as the Knight to that of chivalry. He is too unworldly for the sort of administrative position that might make him prominent and well-to-do, and the only purpose of the benefice that it is suggested he will eventually require will be to sustain him in his chosen calling. Chaucer gives no clear sign of anything but admiration for this figure, but in a post-plague world where there was a desperate need for literate and conscientious parish clergy, the Clerk's remoteness is perhaps open to question. His placing between Merchant and Lawyer is suggestive: while he lacks the typical professional concern for worldly success, he too is a professional, his way of life defined by his specialty. His devotion to logic has perhaps as much in common with that of a modern academic philosopher as with the vocation of the traditional medieval scholar, for whom all study was subordinate to the study of the Bible and the mission of disseminating truth. His speech is steeped in moral virtue, but the famous line that shows him gladly learning and gladly teaching circumscribes that virtue, reminding us that his activity is confined to an academic setting. In the absence of any sure indication of higher purpose, his sheer single-mindedness is potentially as self-interested as the materialism of his fellow-professionals.

The **Man of Law** represents an alternative use of learning: his vast knowledge of law has been devoted to acquiring the robes of the noble clients who retain his services, and gaining title to land on their behalf or his own. More space is devoted to his "purchasing" (acquiring land) than to his administration of justice; and when the narrator notes his "seeming" wisdom and "seeming" busyness we are invited to recognize, as in the portrayal of the Merchant, a façade that conceals self-interest.

The Man of Law is explicitly paired with the **Franklin**, whose status in the social hierarchy was perhaps as ambiguous for fourteenth-century readers as it has proved for modern critics, and whose many important public functions are presented as a sort of appendix to the portrayal of a man who is chiefly programmed by the material demands of his way of life. Such details as his high coloring and the elaborate correlation of his cuisine with the seasons suggest that he is an emblem of hospitality. a sort of Ghost of Christmas Present. But as with the Clerk, there is no affirmation of values to give point to his immersion in the good life, and the emphasis on the occasional nature of his assumption of the roles of "lord and sire" or "knight of the shire," together with the sheer ostentation of his hospitality, hint at a measure of pretension.

In the next few portraits the world of middle-class professionalism is treated more analytically and in a more overtly critical way. The perceptible concern of the lesser gentles to assert their dignity in material terms becomes dominant in the five **Guildsmen**, who illustrate social pretension in an unambiguous form, out of all proportion to their status as craftsmen or City functionaries. Where the clothing of Merchant and Man of Law was merely noted, every detail of the Guildsmen's livery, its newness, workmanship and material, is a claim to status, like the cordovan leather shoes and linen underwear of Sir Thopas. The harmless grandiosity of their ambitions is absorbed and transcended by their wives' desire to become "madame" and be attended like royalty.

This innocent pomposity is oddly juxtaposed with the description of the Guildsmen's **Cook**, the first of Chaucer's grotesques, whose portrait, mainly a dense mass of culinary detail, climaxes with the "mormal" or ulcer on his shin. Such sores were seen as a symptom of lecherous behavior, and the Cook's is no doubt a comment on his character. But after the teasing of the airy pretensions of the Guildsmen, this sudden plunge into crude materiality is also a calculated shock. Translating the conspicuous consumption of the Guildsmen into the gross terms of their food and its preparation, and then inserting into the midst of this confection a memorably vivid emblem of debased self-indulgence, makes us ponder the material basis not only of their aspirations, but of the largesse of the more socially conscious Franklin. The Cook and his sore hint at the powerful satire that is kept at bay by Chaucer's genial equivocations, and anticipate confrontations of churl and gentle in the ordering of the tales.

In the **Shipman** we confront a professionalism devoid of pretension, social or moral. Every detail expresses the practical realities of his engagement with wind and tide, and his frankly predatory relation to commerce. The Shipman's voice is audible in the narrator's account of his lack of scruples, but the effect is not satirical, as in the case of the Monk or Friar, and the narrator's declaration that the Shipman was a "good fellow" expresses not irony but wariness in the presence of one whose dagger is ready to hand.

In contrast to the chilling economy of this portrait, which reduces professionalism to its bare essentials, the elaborate account of the **Physician** conveys a strong suggestion that all his knowledge of ancient medicine and its basis in astronomy and magic, as well as his elaborate repertory of drugs, veils a pseudo-professionalism that seeks to forestall misgivings with a flurry of credentials. Chaucer allows the self-display to proliferate, then steps in to expose the Physician's cold self-interest: his elaborate prescriptions are in marked contrast to his own temperate diet, his richness of dress disguises an habitual parsimony, and an utter lack of religious scruple has enabled him to grow rich in time of plague.

The first dozen lines describing the **Wife of Bath** seem to present a female counterpart to the Guildsmen, proud of her weaving, and eager for such marks of status as immense headdresses, soft leather shoes, and precedence in presenting her offering in church. But as the portrait continues, concern for professional status gives way to a more complex self-assertion. Her dress, conversation, red face, and wide-spaced teeth can be read as signs of a worldly and lustful nature, but her portrait is unique in implying a *self* — not an actual fourteenth-century woman whom Chaucer might have known, but a character whose imperfectly understood desire is to attain recognition as a person, rather than success or status in practical terms. But the prolioferation of her exploits, five marriages and a series of pilgrimages as elaborate as the Knight's campaigns, show this desire to be unfocused, and the narrator confirms this in noting her "wandering by the way." In her we see Chaucer pondering the special dilemma of a woman anxious to claim status and value, yet unable to do so satisfactorily in the terms of precedence and commercial value offered by a male-dominated world. At the same time her endless wandering, and the concluding reference to

the "old dance" of love and its remedies, conjure up the
broader and bleaker vista of a life circumscribed for all
humankind by time and age.

From the complex realism of this portrait we are withdrawn
abruptly to consider the two most idealized figures in the
gallery. The **Parson** exists only as a long celebration of perfect
virtue, and much of the point of his role is in its comprehen-
siveness. A man of learning and a teacher whose actions conform to his words, benign and patient with all yet no respecter
of persons, at once wholly unworldly and astutely aware of
the dangers that beset his flock, he expresses both the con-
templative and the pastoral function of the Church in a way
that Monk, Friar, and Clerk do not. The result of his efforts
is the perfect layman, the **Plowman**, whose labor is wholly
devoted to the Christian community.

That the Parson is set apart from the other clergy suggests
that it is here, among the lower commons and churls, that
such a priest finds his proper task. But Parson and Plowman
are unreal, timeless and virtually disembodied. No detail of
appearance, action or history helps us visualize either one
until, after sixty-five lines of hypothetical perfection, we are
startled by the concluding reference to the Plowman's coat
and horse. Unaffected by the discontents of the actual par-
sons and plowmen of the age, they exist on their own plane,
at a remove from the almost overwhelming realism of the
"churl" group whose portraits conclude the sequence.

The **Miller** is perhaps the lowest in rank of those pilgrims
whose roles are referable to the conventional social hierarchy,
and the one whose portrait is most dominated by sheer
physical presence. Beginning with his great strength and
penchant for violent exercise, we come to center on the particulars of his coarse appearance with a cinematic vividness:

Upon the cop right[1] of his nose he hade   [1] right on the
top

A werte,[1] and theron stood a toft of herys,[2]   [1] wart [2] hairs
Reed[1] as the brustles of a sowes erys;[2]   [1] red [2] ears
His nosethirles[1] blake were and wyde.   [1] nostrils

(I.554–57)

As with the Cook's mormal, one looks for a significance in this emphasis on the grotesque: in terms of medieval physiognomy it may be symptomatic of the Miller's dissolute and shameless character. But his skill in stealing grain, the one occupational trait noted, is coupled with the suggestion that he was honest as millers go, and it seems less a social evil in itself than a symptom of his general lack of restraint. As with the Wife of Bath, his physical and emotional nature is given greater prominence than his externally defined role. At the lower margin of the social order his physical energy, expressed in such actions as the unhinging of doors with his head, assumes an anarchic significance, reminding us of the capacity for random and potentially destructive self-assertion in a society where traditional constraints are being questioned and rejected.

With the **Manciple** we are back in the world of depersonalized greed. As devoid of concrete detail as the Parson's, his portrait consists wholly of the narrator's mock-wonder at his cleverness in exploiting his role as provisioner to a company of lawyers, men far more learned than he, but whom he manages always to keep ahead of in his accounting, presumably by adjusting his records to conceal his embezzling. The meanness of the triumph is the measure of the man: mirrored in the narrator's praise of his cunning is a wholly unreflecting pride in his deception of his learned masters. Petty thievery expresses the measure of his capabilities and aspirations, and his character and world view are wholly defined by it.

The lawyers served by the Manciple are said to be the sort of men who might themselves manage the lands of a great lord. The **Reeve**, though a craftsman rather than a lawyer, has exploited just such a stewardship to his own great profit. His eery power to see through the cunning of others and his stealthy accumulation of riches are really just the trickery of the Manciple writ large, and it is possible to see these two figures, together with the Miller, as forming a kind of grotesque, predatory hierarchy. All three are men of peasant or lower-class origins, and their social status reflects the status of those on whom they feed. The cheerfully unscrupulous Miller is apparently content to engage in give and take with his lower-class clientele (a clientele which, as in the Reeve's tale, doubtless includes Manciples); the Manciple subsists in a constant, parasitic relation to busy professionals, which is itself a sort of lowest-common-denominator profession; and the Reeve, who has abused the trust of his lord, has thereby achieved a purely material ascendancy which represents a perversion of traditional hierarchical values. The physical description of the Reeve, whose gaunt and joyless demeanor and rusty blade are out of keeping with the fine horse and dwelling he has acquired, suggests the final joylessness of a pursuit whose only real consequence is the diminishment of the common good.

The Summoner and the Pardoner, clearly the undesirables of the group, nonetheless have a bizarre vitality which is treated with a certain sympathy, and we come close to them as human beings. The **Summoner**'s face burns like a Cherub's, but while the Cherub's glows with constant love of God, the Summoner is burned by vice and a terrible need for human contact. The damning concrete details of his portrait are often at odds with the emphasis of the narrator's account of him. The skin condition that makes children fear to look at him is no doubt a sign of depravity, but Chaucer lets the physical details speak for themselves, while dwelling on the desperate energy of the Summoner's attempts at conviviality, his singing and clowning, and his pathetic pretence of speaking Latin. As the equivalent for the ecclesiastical court of a modern server of writs, his profession was proverbial for petty corruption, and it is therefore notable that Chaucer emphasizes, not the monetary, but the social aspect of his role. We never see him extort money, but we do hear him seeking to ingratiate himself with those to whom he should be threatening punishment; a willing drinking companion may enjoy his mistress in peace, and in the presence of such a "good fellow" the Summoner speaks with an almost disarming candor about the mercenary motives behind the Archdeacon's decrees of excommunication. If we are uneasy

at his confidential relations with young people, it is likely that
he has exercised his "daunger" (power) to make himself privy
to their affairs out of vicarious identification rather than for
gain.

Whatever homosexual overtones may be present in the
companionship of Summoner and Pardoner and the love
song they sing in harmony, these are also emblematic of the
deeper common need of men who are chronically isolated,
both by the suspect nature of their professions and by personal traits for which they are not fully accountable. The
Pardoner's response to isolation is a defiant exhibitionism.
His self-advertising dress and manner are enhanced by the
narrator's report of his success in duping rural congregations
with false relics and dubious powers of absolution, which he
sells for his own profit on the strength of his flamboyant
preaching and his authority, presumably sanctioned by the
Church, as a distributor of "pardons." But the Pardoner's
physical appearance tells a different story. His hare's eyes,
perhaps symbolic of lechery, are also those of a small animal
at bay, and the narrator's guileless comments on the outward
signs of an apparently congenital sterility are painfully drawn
out. His remarks on the wallet in the Pardoner's lap, full of
pardons newly arrived, "all hot," from Rome, point to the
contrast between the Pardoner's physical deficiency and the
substitute potency of his credentials. The lines are as close as
the narrator ever comes to joking about something a pilgrim
cannot help, and hint at the sort of meanness that continually
threatens such a figure in the world at large. Together,
Pardoner and Summoner show us professional greed in its
lowest form, reinforced by a ruthless exploitation of the
authority of the Church and accompanied by vivid suggestions
of personal corruption. As such they bring Chaucer's anatomy
of a society in flux to an appropriately ominous conclusion.
But they also remind us that the world of the *Canterbury Tales*
is already a cruel world, one that creates victims and stigmatizes
aberrant behavior without regard to the human needs that
drive even the most corrupt human beings.

Having completed his survey of the pilgrims, and before

going on to develop his narrative, the narrator offers a curious apology:

> But first I pray yow, of youre curteisye,
> That ye n'arette[1] it to my vileynye,[2]
>
> [1] impute
> [2] low behavior
>
> Thogh that I pleynly speke in this mateere,
> To telle yow hir wordes and hir cheere.[1]
>
> [1] appearance
>
> (I.725–28)

The rhyme "curteisye / vileinye" is significant. The narrator concedes that his enterprise will involve a measure of "villainy," anti-courtly behavior which he must report faithfully or falsify his material. In appealing to our courtesy he is not just preserving the fiction of the courtly poet addressing a genteel audience, but asking us to exercise forbearance and good will in the face of the unavoidable vulgarity of his material, and thereby to preserve a decorum he himself has been forced to abandon. In self-defense he notes that Christ spoke "broadly" (freely, plainly) in the Gospels, clearly with no base intention, and cites Plato's assertion that words must reflect the character of what they represent. But the utter inappropriateness of the allusions only makes more plain his haplessness in the face of the task he has recklessly undertaken. Plato's maxim about language occurs in the course of a discussion of the difficulty of adapting human language to the representation of the unchanging reality of the divine, whereas Chaucer's narrator is attempting to deal with precisely that which resists the stability of ideal paradigms. Christ's homely sayings and examples gave definition and orientation to the aspirations of countless multitudes, but the narrator is trying to adapt his linguistic medium to the divergent impulses of a random collection of complex individuals. His very appropriation of the Platonic formula is a perversion of the hierarchy he seeks so desperately to maintain, and he finally acknowledges his difficulty outright, concluding his apology by admitting that he may, through lack of wit, have failed to arrange his pilgrims according to their "degree" or social rank. He is suspended between the ordering decorum of the courtly tradition, a standard of beauty, value, and order he cannot maintain, and a world of specious gentility and encroaching "villainy" which threatens to engulf him and his work. In a world where so many forms of "worthiness" abound, where the Friar is "virtuous" and the Manciple and Pardoner are "gentil," it is impossible to ensure that words are "cousin" (i.e. related) to what they would represent: language threatens to become as valueless as the Summoner's shield made out of a cake.

At this point the narrator introduces the **Host**, Harry Baily, who quickly generates a convivial atmosphere and assumes the role of guide and master of the revels to the company. In approving his proposal of a tale-telling contest with a meal as the prize, the pilgrims relegate pilgrimage to the background, in favor of a competition all too true to the daily life implied by the gallery of portraits. Harry is scrupulous in respecting those he considers his social superiors, and hence a limited hierarchy and an intermittent courtesy are maintained. But his ascendancy marks the final stage of the narrator's abrogation of responsibility for the conduct of the story. Though the luck of the draw (doubtless obsequiously rigged by Harry) assigns the first tale to the Knight, it has been made elaborately clear that the subsequent proceedings will have a life of their own; any order we are able, "of our curteisye," to detect in them will be a product of interactions that have little to do with traditional social values.

Chapter 3

Gentles: chivalry and the courtly world

If the attributes of Chaucer's Knight are conventional and old-fashioned, his chivalric values nonetheless provided a standard that was constantly invoked in the later fourteenth century. The workings of royal power were being scrutinized by an increasingly self-assertive Commons, but the essentially personal and apolitical ideals of chivalry still provided a model of kingship: Edward III won fame as a soldier in the French campaigns of the 1340s, and his foundation of the Order of the Garter defined the loyalty of worthy knights by linking it to an institution of soldiers with the King at its head, established as the highest embodiment of chivalric values. Chivalry also had a domestic side, as the Squire's portrait reminds us. Courtesy, and especially the courtesy of lovers, was part of the definition of the perfect knight. But the relationship of love and war is one-sided: honoring his lady confirms the knight's courtesy, but it is most of all an excuse for the self-centered enterprise of demonstrating prowess. In practice, warfare remains the true test of chivalry, and courtesy is largely the stuff of courtly poetry.

The lack of correspondence between the values proper to active chivalry and those of courtly society in its domestic aspect is a central concern in those of the *Canterbury Tales* that deal with the aristocratic world. The Knight's tale is intended to affirm the ordering power of chivalry, but as it proceeds chivalry comes to seem an unwieldy means of regulating human life, its laws and rituals all too easily undermined by the martial force that is its ultimate *raison d'être*. The Squire's view of the world is circumscribed by his infatuation with the courtly life: chivalry is reduced to random adventure, almost to sheer novelty, and social relations are essentially an occasion for the display of fine feeling. The Franklin's tale addresses the relations of the courtly and chivalric worlds directly, testing the capacity of courtly values to mediate the relations of men governed by the code of chivalry with women who are the exalted objects of courtly reverence, but whose real status is determined by male prerogatives and male honor.

The central figure in the Knight's tale is Theseus, Duke of Athens. The tale traces the linked fortunes of the Theban princes Palamon and Arcite as rivals for the hand of the Amazon Emily, but the action takes place at Theseus' court and under his presiding authority, and he embodies chivalric heroism in its highest form. The Knight opens with a review of Theseus' heroic exploits, reduced to occasions for praise of his hero. Theseus' conquest of the Amazons and his ensuing marriage to the Amazon queen Ypolita are barely noted, but there is space for a sort of running gloss on the wisdom, chivalry, glory, and nobility displayed by Theseus during the campaign. A still briefer account of Theseus' intervention to end the bloody war between Argos and Thebes includes vivid glimpses of his banner and crest, shows him slaying Creon "manly as a knight," and is reported from beginning to end as if Theseus had accomplished it single-handed. Between these two summaries, the narrative slows and dilates to show Theseus responding magnanimously to the appeal of the widows of the Greek warriors who lie unburied at Thebes. The episode becomes a sort of ikon of knightly responsibility, set off by the flanking reports of Theseus' virtues in action as if by a triumphal arch.

Theseus will make several such emblematic appearances in the course of the tale: intervening to suspend the conflict between Palamon and Arcite; defining the rules of the great tournament which is to resolve the issue between the lovers; ordering the funeral of Arcite; and finally invoking the First Mover to renew his people's faith in Providence. These authoritative gestures are the essence of the story for the Knight, an expression of the highest ambition of medieval culture in its secular aspect, transforming classical heroism into a chivalry that combines valor in war with political

responsibility and courtly grace. The Knight is at once the in-
stigator of the tale and an enthusiastic member of the audience,
unquestioning of the values of his protagonists. When he tells
us that Theseus conquered the Amazons by virtue of "his
wisdom and his chivalry," he means just what he says. He
endorses Theseus' every decision, and approves his lavish
expenditure on public spectacles. He thinks fighting for a lady
is "a lusty sight for to see," and his account of the great and
fatal tournament which climaxes the poem is that of an insider
addressing an audience of aficionados.

But this optimism cannot conceal the increasing grimness of
the story that unfolds. As Palamon and Arcite compete for
the hand of Ypolita's sister Emily, the order created by Theseus
to contain and resolve their conflict proves inadequate to the
task. The conventions of courtly romance are present: Emily
performs the rites of a courtly girlhood, and we see her in the
garden setting of love-allegory, ripe for discovery by a young
man who might through ritual service win her favor, as both
Palamon and Arcite propose to do, but no such event takes
place. Emily is seen from afar, not by one, but by two lovers.
Each goes through the posturings of the love-struck courtier
in isolation, but neither can declare himself; they remain trap-
ped in the violent world of heroic legend, and must fight one
another rather than appeal to the favor of Emily in order to
win her. Yet this mortal hatred, and apparently inescapable
legacy of Thebes, is at the same time the essence of the chivalric
life, as Chaucer reminds us in various ways. Even in the crucial
forest episode, when both are seized by raging jealousy and
on the point of fighting to the death, chivalry remains an essential part of their behavior; the two knights behave with
meticulous courtesy, helping each other to arm before charg-
ing into a battle which quickly reduces both to wild beasts.
Theseus, too, sees their conflict in chivalric terms. Coming
upon them ankle-deep in their own blood, he is induced to spare
them on the grounds that both are gentle, and their conflict
"no thing but for love." Characteristically he recognizes love's
violent effects, but responds with wry, almost sarcastic humor,
taking for granted that this is the way of the chivalric world:

Thus hath hir[1] lord, the god of love, ypayed   [1] their
Hir wages and hir fees for hir servyse!

(I.1801–2)

The Knight himself is equally unquestioning of his characters' commitment to chivalry, but he grows steadily more puzzled and dogged as the story becomes harder to control, and his investment in Theseus' attempt to reduce conflict to ritual is dramatized with increasing urgency. Just as he makes us aware of the resources deployed by Theseus, the expenditure, the recruitment of technical and artistic expertise, and the ideological promotion by which he attempts to resolve the Theban dilemma that has erupted in his Athens, so Chaucer calls attention to the mechanics of compression and dilation, closure and renewal by which the Knight seeks to control his narrative. The tournament and its tragic aftermath bring these parallel projects to a new crisis: the Knight discovers in spite of himself realities which the ideology and literary conventions of chivalry tend to deny, and is forced to acknowledge the primitive forces that inform even the most exalted forms of the chivalric code.

As the Knight's narrative performance proceeds, moreover, his own experience is brought strikingly to the fore. We see this first in his long, digressive account of the interiors of the three temples erected in honor of Venus, Mars, and Diana on the perimeter of Theseus' great stadium, where a tournament is to resolve the lovers' dispute, and again in his powerful and powerfully motivated account of the funeral of Arcite. In describing the temples the Knight seems to lose control of his material: created to celebrate the gods, the temples show their influence at its most malign. The sphere of Venus as depicted on the walls of her shrine is a world of violent feeling, intrigue, and continual restless movement; the love-idealism proper to chivalry is recalled only in a few incidental details. A vast painting in the temple of Mars shows not only the ruin and slaughter of war, but a violence that pervades all life, from the treachery of the back streets to such ordinary tasks as cooking, keeping pigs, driving carts; the work of barber, butcher, and smith.

By exposing the sheer unwieldy power of the gods, the two temples express the Knight's dawning awareness of the complexity of the world he seeks to order, and perhaps also an awareness that his warrior's vocation has not fully prepared him to deal with the sophistication and diversity of this world. But in the temple of Diana the Knight encounters something wholly new. The recurring theme of the representations on its walls is the story "of huntyng and of shamefast chastitee," and the paratactic relation of the two terms expresses the ambiguous character of a sexual tension that goes back to the beginnings of mythic history. Here the Knight beholds Callisto, Actaeon, and other victims of Diana's militant and vengeful chastity, and we may see him beginning to discover, involuntarily and without recognizing it, his own anxiety in the face of the feminine will — something hardly acknowledged by chivalry, imperfectly assimilated to the chivalric vision of life, and hence little more than a vaguely imagined source of potential violence. As he discovers his own dark fears at the heart of the creation which was to express his faith and pride in chivalric order, he resembles strikingly the figure in whom the primal hostility of female autonomy to male encroachment expresses itself most powerfully — the hunter Actaeon, turned to a stag and torn apart by his own hounds for having unintentionally beheld the naked goddess. The encounter of Actaeon and Diana seems to define the Knight's vision of the goddess herself, seated on the back of a stag and surrounded by hounds. The confrontation defines a barrier: the Knight is as close as his chivalric sensibility can attain to recognizing the limited nature of his masculine vision, and the social and sexual tensions generated by its presumption to order human life.

The same sense that the Knight is on the point of awakening to a new reality is present as he describes the funeral of Arcite. Subject to a complex therapy by the need to recount this event, he is compelled to acknowledge, all the while denying his impulse to do so, a sense of horror and compassion in the face of death. The Knight emphasizes the official character of the event and dwells on its sumptuousness, but the ritual has a life of its own, and draws him into an involuntary identification with his characters. The elaborate rhetorical gesture whereby he declines to describe Arcite's cremation, only to have the details of the event force their way into his consciousness in spite of his attempt to exclude them, shows him succumbing to the sheer primitive power of the ceremony. As Arcite's funeral pyre is strewn with jewels, arms, and sumptuous clothing, the pretensions of chivalry are laid aside: for a moment the Knight appears as a warrior pure and simple, honoring a fallen comrade in a spirit closer to the world of *Beowulf* or Homer than to the confections of romance. Civilization itself is reduced to the primordial clearing of the forest, and the trappings of courtly life become mere talismans, an offering to the dark powers that govern the fortunes of life and war.

The funeral passage is a new departure in other ways as well. A passive, placatory ritual is substituted for the posturings of active chivalry. The naming of the types of tree that form the pyre, and the vivid imagining of the terror of animals and forest spirits "disinherited" by the clearing of the forest, point to the desecration inseparable from the rite being enacted. We are also made aware of the situation of the shocked and bewildered Emily, whose presence is all the more vivid for the restraint with which the Knight declines to describe her swoon as the flames arise, "ne what she spak, ne what was hir desir." Though the Knight never abandons chivalric decorum, we sense that he has again come close to acknowledging the fundamental limitations of the code by which he lives.

But the Knight's purpose is finally political, and it is important to remember that the sort of public display his tale depicts had great political significance in fourteenth-century England. As Anne Middleton observes, such spectacles led people to participate willingly in rituals that expressed the "entente" of their ruler, thereby affirming the ruler's prowess in aesthetic terms. Chaucer's larger project in the tale is a testing of this aesthetic control, and by implication a testing of the power of authoritarian chivalry to engage and control the tensions of a restive and dynamic society. The Knight labors to present the exercise of power in a positive light, but the tale's most memorable image of it is Saturn, the eldest of the gods, who undertakes to reconcile the conflict of Venus and Mars over the fates of Palamon and Arcite, and in the process provides a grim account of a universe over which he claims absolute power. Saturn's "authority" encompasses

The fallynge of the toures[1] and of the walles	[1] towers
Upon the mynour[1] or the carpenter.	[1] miner
I slow[1] Sampsoun, shakynge the piler,[2]	[1] slew [2] pillar
And myne be the maladyes colde,	
The derke tresons, and the castes[1] olde;	[1] plans, plots
My lookyng is the fader[1] of pestilence.	[1] father

(I.2464–69)

The speech recalls that in which the Jupiter of Vergil's *Aeneid* assures Venus that her son Aeneas will become the father of an empire without end, a prophecy complemented by the great simile that compares Neptune, calming the storm of the poem's opening episode, to a Roman statesman quelling sedition by his eloquence and authority. But Saturn's universe is "governed" only by force, so ruthlessly imposed and so wholly alien to the world it dominates that plague and social rebellion appear as equally natural consequences of the pressure it exerts. Precisely at the center of Saturn's speech, and so at the center of his concentric universe, is Samson, a hero from another tradition, a dedicated man with a will and mission of his own. But the Knight's political vision allows us no sure sense of relation to Samson in this context; his presence points up the basic mindlessness of Saturn's universe, but Samson himself remains enigmatic, an image of ultimate freedom or ultimate futility.

The confidence of Theseus and his narrator has been shaken, but their political duty does not cease. In the subdued atmosphere of the tale's final episode we see Theseus less as hero than as statesman. Resolving to bring about a marriage between Palamon and Emily, he justifies his decision with a long discourse on the order of things, but the marriage is clearly a political event, designed to preserve the subordination of Thebes to Athens. The speech, too, must be seen as a political act, and not as providing a serious philosophical perspective on the story. It begins by asserting that a bond of love orders the universe, preserving harmony and imposing a fixed term on existence: everything that lives must die. From this unarguable fact Theseus argues the stability, purposefulness, and benevolence of Jupiter, the universal "prince and cause," but the force of the speech derives wholly from the need to rationalize the fact of our mortality. In effect death becomes the sole basis for affirming the purpose of life. Theseus bids his auditors put the best face on the inevitable, and discovers Providence in the fact that Arcite was cut down at the height of his vigor and renown, removed from the "foule prisoun" of life before his name could be dimmed by age.

The speech makes disconcertingly clear the limited scope of Theseus' power to create order, but as a political gesture it is enlightened and courageous. The conqueror whose chivalry had once seemed all-sufficient has been humbled, but can still exert his authority to effect marriage and decree a general festivity, thus satisfying the formal requirements of romance and enlisting his subjects in the cause of preserving order by a ceremonial affirmation of love and loyalty. And in Theseus' final gestures we may discern the Knight, too, making an appeal comparable to that with which Chaucer himself ends the General Prologue. In both cases the best of intentions have been subverted by the sheer disorderliness of life, and both Chaucer and the Knight solicit the courtesy of their hearers to acknowledge and vindicate their good faith.

For the Knight, the very survival of social order depends on the success of the chivalric enterprise. The Squire's tale, however, dramatizes a sensibility for which courtliness is an end in itself. His naive enthusiasm is appealing, but his tale exposes his arbitrary assumption of the social superiority of court culture, and calls into question the ethical values of his courtly idealism. For the Squire courtly values are virtually interchangeable in those who possess them, and the first seventy-five lines of his tale do little more than demonstrate this fact.

King Cambuskyan has ruled for twenty years and has a son of marriageable age, yet he is "yong" and "fressh." Canacee is beautiful and a princess, and so is necessarily virtuous and compassionate. This system of values is never examined. The sudden entry of a knight on a horse of brass is only a momentary diversion for Cambuskyan's courtiers, and does not, like the similar intrusion in *Sir Gawain and the Green Knight*, lead to a testing confrontation with a larger, more complex world.

Vacuous in itself, the idealizing tone of the romance is constantly marred by oddly mundane details. We can accept Canacee's early departure from a feast without being told that like most women, she was not a heavy drinker. We may or may not be moved when the princess weeps as if she would turn to water over the tale of a lovelorn falcon, but it is simply funny when the bird suddenly tells her to be quiet. The Squire concludes Cambuskyan's feast with a clinical discourse on the "fumositee" that confuses the dreams of those who have been drinking, and provides a similar scientific gloss on the morning haze in which Canacee meets her falcon, but there is no hint as to why he introduces these prosaic matters. He elsewhere asserts an aristocratic disdain for such matter-of-factness, sneering at the conjectures of the common people as to the nature of the horse of brass, which is too "subtle" for their ignorance to grasp; but in fact many of their speculations are rather sophisticated, being based on a knowledge of "olde poetries" of Perseus and the fall of Troy, and there is nothing in the poem to refute their more down-to-earth suspicion that the horse is a mere conjurer's trick. Later, moreover, the Squire describes the court as equally agog, and in the event nothing could be less subtle than the stranger knight's demonstration of how the horse may be activated by the twirling of a set of little pins. By the time it unexpectedly vanishes, the Squire seems to have lost interest in it ("ye get namoore of me"). Impervious to humor or irony, his imaginings have no rationale beyond the desire for novelty, and he can descend to the banal details of digestion or machinery with no sense of incongruity. For the Knight, the ordinary world was the temple of Mars, a threat to courtly decorum which it was the duty of chivalry to contain or suppress. The Squire's shiftings between courtly fantasy and mundane reality give rise to no such tension because there is nothing at stake.

The idyll of Canacee and the falcon withdraws us from this cluttered scene to the beauty and apparent seriousness of a discourse on the gentle heart, which sees a "similitude" of itself in the plight of those who suffer:

> For gentil herte kitheth[1] gentilesse.   [1] displays
> I se wel that ye han[1] of my distres   [1] have
> Compassion, my faire Canacee,
> Of verray[1] wommanly benignytee   [1] true
> That Nature in youre principles hath set.
>
> (V.483–87)

Here the idealism seems real, and this higher note is sustained in the falcon's account of how her pure feelings were exploited by a faithless tercelet (young male falcon): her will became "his willes instrument," and by her betrayal she understands the pain of death.

The idea that the gentle heart is especially accessible to pity occurs frequently in Chaucer's poetry, but it is a perilously ambiguous notion, and can seem to imply that the capacity for love or compassion is a function of the tastes and values of the nobly born. The falcon's story points up this ambiguity, for the tercelet who deceived her was not only "gentil born," but "welle of alle gentilesse" in his behavior, master of the words that express "gentilesse of love." Now she knows the emptiness of mere breeding; when the allure of "newfangelnesse" causes lovers' feelings to alter: "No gentilesse of blood ne may hem bynde." Thus the net effect of her discourse is to remind us that gentility has no intrinsic value, and it provides a salutary comment on the emptiness of the Squire's earlier celebration of courtly life.

What the episode means to the Squire is harder to tell. He narrates it well, but we should also note the zeal with which, having brought it to a close, he launches at once into an elaborate preview of coming attractions. His infatuation with romance has clearly survived his exposure to the falcon's hard-earned wisdom, and he remains as open to "new fangelnesse" as any young man or bird. As he elsewhere modestly hints, he is also, like the false tercelet, an adept in the rituals of "love and his servyse." We may ask whether the eloquence with which he endows the falcon is not simply a virtuoso exercise in the rhetoric of *gentilesse*, a cultivation of fine feelings for their own sake.

Even on its own terms, moreover, the courtly rhetoric of the falcon's discourse is disoriented and arbitrary. To explain her lover's infidelity, Canacee employs an elaborate simile which compares the errant bird, rather confusingly, to a bird: as a caged bird, however gently treated, will always long to escape, and will give up a diet of milk and honey in favor of eating worms in the wild, so the tercelet, reverting to his natural bent, pursued a new love. For Boethius, the source of this simile, such avian behavior illustrates a profound truth, the impulse of all creatures to realize their natural roles in an ultimately divine order. But for the falcon, it illustrates only a repudiation of virtue in response to the appeal of novelty. The simile in its new context is not inappropriate, but its meaning is sharply attenuated: a bird fails to appreciate the natural truth at the heart of a bird-simile. The paradox illustrates the danger of viewing life through the haze of the Squire's courtly vision: a world confected entirely out of the values and trappings of courtliness can become itself a cage, divorced from reality like the beautiful birdhouse Canacee creates for the falcon, its walls inscribed with cautionary but essentially meaningless images of avian infidelity. In such a world, where everything is traeted with equal seriousness, nothing can finally be taken seriously.

But the Squire is very young, and as he declares, his will is good. Chaucer's essential sympathy is expressed by the Franklin, who interrupts the too-ambitious narrative with tactful praise of its eloquence, and prefaces his own tale by apologizing for his lack of rhetorical skill. In place of the Squire's hermetic world, where values, rhetoric and nature are assumed to be in harmony, the Franklin announces a world where things are either real or artificial. His tale, borrowed from the "gentle Britons" of old, will be courtly. But like the Franklin himself, whose sumptuous style of life has not precluded the performance of important public duties, it will never lose touch with the world of the everyday.

At first glance the Franklin's long opening account of the courtship of Dorigen and Arveragus is informed by the sort of idealizing zeal the Squire might have bestowed on the wooing of Canacee. The demands of courtly love-service are fully satisfied, and delicate questions of "soveraynetee," "suffrance" and "libertee," sources of deep sexual tension elsewhere in the *Tales*, are discussed openly and at length by the two lovers, who reach a "humble, wys accord." Only after some seventy lines of affirmation does the Franklin hint at a more detached perspective:

> Who koude¹ telle, but² he hadde wedded   ¹ could ² unless
>   be,³   ³ been
> The joye, the ese, and the prosperitee
> That is bitwixe¹ an housbonde and his wyf?   ¹ between
> A yeer and moore lasted this blisful lyf.
>   (V.803–6)

Only the Merchant's January could speak so broadly of the bliss of marriage with a straight face, and when the Franklin ends by asserting that the idyll lasted an entire year, he is telling us that it was too good to be true, a tour de force of courtly convention. A moment later one convention abruptly gives place to another, as Arveragus leaves to spend two years tourneying in England, showing a proper knightly concern for honor, but at the same time following his "lust" as readily as the Squire's faithless tercelet. He will return, and his fidelity is never questioned, but the freedom with which he comes and goes and his absorption in his own knightly pursuits will be called into question.

During much of the tale we view the world through the eyes of Dorigen. She too has a sense of honor, and her marriage is clearly the central fact in her life. But she is also, like Arveragus, constrained by her role: she is female courtliness itself, for whom life is a continuous response to the prompting of courtly convention. Finding herself in the situation of the abandoned heroine, she grieves, sincerely but conventionally, "As doon thise noble wyves whan hem liketh." Concerned friends seek to console her, but though they offer a rational perspective, their efforts also enhance her status as the central figure in a courtly love-drama. We see her in a series of sentimental poses amid landscapes ranging from the grim Breton coast to a beautiful garden, all of which only remind her poignantly of her absent lord. A tendency to organize the universe around herself and her sorrow becomes explicit in her soliloquy as she contemplates the rocky coast. She refuses to make virtue of necessity by accepting the rocks as part of the divine order, but sees them as a "foul confusion," an irrational element in a universe which should be a beautiful setting for the lives of beautiful people.

So conditioned are Dorigen's thoughts by convention that when the squire Aurelius, fresher than the month of May, surfaces among dancers in a paradisal garden and reveals his passion, her real but subjective concern for Arveragus adapts itself all too readily to the courtly context. She first firmly rebuffs Aurelius; but then, "in play," she promises her love if he will rid the coast of the rocks which threaten Arveragus' safe return, translating her fantasy of altering nature on his behalf into a bargain with her importunate suitor, a game which will eventually lead her to thoughts (albeit highly conventional thoughts) of suicide.

Aurelius exists only to play the lovesick squire, and seeks to adapt the universe to his needs as a matter of course. Like Dorigen, he constantly invokes universal powers, but while Dorigen's oaths reveal the vestiges of sound instinct, those of Aurelius express only his dislocation from reality. He affirms God's authorship of the world even as he wishes himself out of it; later in the tale his scorn at the news that the removal of the rocks by magic will cost him a thousand pounds he does not possess is couched in the magnificent vagueness of an oath by "This wyde world, which that men saye is round." Rejected by Dorigen, he falls ill for two years, and the unreality in which he languishes is sharply contrasted with the concrete world of Arveragus, who returns home in the meantime, so sure of his position as to be incapable of imagining another man's address to his wife, and immediately restores Dorigen to her proper sphere.

At this point, the radical separation of squire and lady is bridged by magic. In the long central portion of the story, dominated by detailed descriptions of the workings and effects of "artes that been curious," the seemingly impossible removal of the rocks seemingly comes to pass, and Dorigen is confronted with a moral crisis brought about, as she recognizes, "against the process of nature," though it never occurs to her to question the reality of the rocks' disappearance. The crisis is brought on by "appearance," an illusion seemingly little different from those effected as entertainment by conjurers, but the Franklin makes the magical element in his story an occasion for introducing more significant matters.

In the study of the clerk whose powers he enlists, Aurelius is shown a series of magical tableaux. He first beholds a park full of deer:

> He saugh[1] of them an hondred slayn with
> > houndes,   [1] saw
> And somme with arwes[1] blede of bittre
> > woundes.   [1] arrows
> He saugh, whan voyded[1] were thise wilde
> > deer,   [1] removed
> Thise fauconers upon a fair ryver,
> That with hir haukes han[1] the heron slayn.   [1] had
> Tho[1] saugh he knyghtes justyng[2] in a playn;   [1] then [2] jousting
> And after this he dide hym swich[1] plesaunce   [1] such
> That he hym shewed[1] his lady on a daunce,   [1] showed
> On which hymself he daunced, as hym
> > thoughte.
> > (V.1193–1201)

Even as they gratify Aurelius' all too impressionable fantasy, the tableaux are the Franklin's shrewd comment on the world of his poem. The series of interactions of strength and beauty, in which violence is refined and ritualized but not essentially transformed, is a panorama of knightly life, the life lived eagerly and successfully by Arveragus. The tableaux suggest its predatory character, and the progression from hunt to joust hints at its inherent tendency to cultivate conflict for its own sake. The world of Aurelius' love, the social world where the relations of men and women are formed by courtly values, is set apart, and the unresolved juxtaposition of the chivalric and the courtly is an emblem of the flawed social values operative in the world of the tale. It exposes the self-absorption of the chivalric life, a failure to assimilate social values which will be exposed in Arveragus' attempts to deal with the consequences of Dorigen's rash promise. At the same time the placement of the vision of dancing lovers as the climax of the spectacle suggests the intensity of Aurelius' obsession. It recalls the attempts of Dorigen's friends to console her by exposing her to ongoing natural life, attempts which had only made her more aware of her status as a courtly heroine. If Arveragus is destined to show himself obtuse and uncertain in the face of social crisis, Aurelius and Dorigen, left to their own courtly devices, are children, their sense of social reality wholly determined by their own hopes and fears.

In contrast, and as a proem to the conjuring away of the rocks, the Franklin recalls us to the natural world. It is December. Frost has blighted the green world, and human life has withdrawn indoors:

> Janus sit by the fyr, with double berd,[1]   [1] beard
> And drynketh of his bugle horn the wyn;
> Biforn hym stant[1] brawen[2] of the tusked   [1] stands [2] flesh
>   swyn,[3]   [3] swine, boar
> And "Nowel" crieth every lusty man.
>   (V.1252–55)

The seasonal festival, incorporating the implements and trophies of the hunt into a celebration that makes the cycle of life and death a source of continuity and renewal, reminds us of the lack of real purpose in the lives of the protagonists. But there is a further reason for asserting the bond between man and nature at this point: for the curiously unmagical account of the clerk's magic, which follows immediately, is as much an assertion of sympathy with nature as Janus' festival. Its emphasis is not on what the clerk effects, but on the knowledge his work requires. His books and instruments are the tools, not of illusion, but of scientific investigation. The Franklin mutters about "juggling" and "heathen" tricks, but what we actually see is an astronomer determining by observation that certain phenomena are likely to occur. Some thirty lines are devoted to the clerk's studies, and when the time is right, the rocks seem for "a week or two" to be gone. We are told that this occurs through magic, but in the knowledge the clerk deploys there is no trace of the occult. His sympathy with nature is to mere "juggling" as the functional rituals of the hunt to Arveragus' joustings, or as real marriage to the idyllic fantasies of Aurelius.

As the story nears its crisis, the unreality of the protagonists' lives becomes steadily more plain. When Aurelius reports the disappearance of the rocks to Dorigen, it is as though he wished it had not happened. He speaks "With dreadful heart," refers seven times to the death she has it in her power to inflict on him, and shows no hint of passion. The operatic soliloquy in which Dorigen resolves to evade the imagined threat to her wifely honor through suicide is equally ineffectual. The fateful decision is announced early on, and the ninety lines that follow − a list of women who took their own lives rather than surrender their chastity − serve only to allow Dorigen's image of herself to assume tragic proportions, and to keep death at bay by sheer verbosity until Arveragus' timely return.

Arveragus' conduct is harder to gauge. His first reaction to his wife's anxiety is calm, even amused, but he ends in tears, bidding her keep her compact with Aurelius, but adding the shocking command that she keep the affair a secret "on pain of death." This shift from a cheerful optimism like the Franklin's own to a tyrant-like assertion of authority, capped by the noble declaration "Trouthe [i.e. a promise, one's word] is the hyeste thyng that man may kepe," has been variously explained: as expressing Arveragus' pain at the decision he must make; as a shrewd manipulation of Dorigen; as a sign of perplexity or moral confusion. But it remains

opaque, psychologically and morally, and perhaps its main
purpose is to make us question the Franklin's earlier emphasis
on the trust central to this marriage. In this first testing of the
relationship Arveragus all too readily assumes the role of
domestic tyrant, and any nobility we may discern in his insistence on the importance of keeping troth is compromised
by our awareness that he is treating his own marriage and
Aurelius' fantastically contrived idyll with equal seriousness.

For all their elaborate pledges to one another, Arveragus
and Dorigen move in separate spheres, one wholly concerned
with masculine endeavor and honor, the other devoted to exaltation and indulgence of the feminine. These worlds have
different standards; they belong, as it were, to different
genres. When Arveragus is asked to judge by the standards of
active chivalry a problem arising in the narcissistic world of
courtly play, where the articulation of imagined desire is an
end in itself and action is always deferred, his chivalry
becomes a blunt instrument, and his attempt to interpret the
situation ethically founders in contradiction. Aurelius, too, is
daunted by the exposure of his fantasy to reality, and at
Dorigen's first "alas! alas!" he is disarmed once and for all.
For both knight and squire, the gesture of renunciation that
is explained as *gentilesse* is really an acknowledgment of their
inadequacy to the demands of a situation whose absurdity is
a consequence of their own self-indulgent idealism.

But the tale is crowned by the clerk-magician's refusal to
claim payment for his work, and it ends with the Franklin's
demand that we compare his gentle deed with the renun-
ciatory gestures of Arveragus and Aurelius. The world of
courtly values, menaced by the harsh reality of Aurelius' un-
payable debt, is preserved by a gratuitous generosity that *but clerk*
reminds us of the precariousness, but at the same time the *too many*
necessity, of *gentilesse* in all human relations. Once again we *not have been*
are made to recall the narrator's appeal at the end of the *generous*
General Prologue. In themselves courtly values are inadequate to the task of ordering social reality, but without
courtesy the social world becomes chaotic and inhuman.

Chapter 4

Churls: commerce and the material world

When the drunken Miller intrudes on the Host's attempt to order the sequence of tale-telling with his "legend" of a carpenter and his wife, his purpose is to "quite" or "repay" the Knight's tale. He responds as a "churl" to a tale of upper-class manners and values, and the bawdy energy of his performance is in itself an apt comment on the Knight's abstract and ritualized universe. It is an essentially conservative response: the Miller offers no alternative to a social structure in which churls and gentles have their proper stations. But his tale sets a complex process in motion. As we move forward through the increasingly violent give-and-take of the Reeve's fabliau to the Cook's world of anarchic self-indulgence, hierarchy is abandoned, and as the poem proceeds it becomes hard to discern any such clear-cut opposition of values as that between Knight and Miller.

The tellers of the tales to be discussed in this chapter, though they include the gentle Merchant and worthy Friar, can all be called "churls." Their viewpoint is materialistic and amoral but, with no regard for orthodox social and religious values, they exhibit a strong, unwieldy aptitude for social criticism. Nearly all their tales are comic, but their lives and the lives of their characters are often so distorted by ambition, the commercializing of social relations, or the bitterness of empty old age as to make it impossible for them to pursue even the elemental goods of food, drink, and sex in a straightforward way. They force us to envision a society cut off from its sustaining bonds by rampant individualism to the point of losing the capacity for love.

The Miller is the most genial of the churls, and the vehicle

of his criticism is parody, aimed at the Knight's treatment of
his love story. He balances the chivalry of Arcite with the
aggressive ingenuity of the student Nicholas, and like the
Knight, responding to Theseus' tournament, he pays his poor
clerk the hero's tribute of alliteration, describing how love of
his "lemman" (sweetheart) makes him "hold her hard by the
haunchbones." The skittish dandyism of Absolon, which
gives way so abruptly and unexpectedly to violent action,
recalls the uneasy relation of religiosity and reckless anger in
Palamon. And the stereotypical Emily is eclipsed by the vivid
description of Alisoun, a superb parody of courtly rhetoric in
which the details of form and attire, far from reducing her
charms to emblems of modesty and virtue, focus our interest
on her lively physical presence. For the Knight's aristocratic
idealism the Miller substitutes a more prosaic sense of the
prerogatives of nobility: Alisoun is one "For any *lord* to leg-
gen (lay) in his bedde, / Or yet for any good *yeman* to
wedde." Nicholas' wooing of her deflates the conventions of
courtly love:

> This Nicholas gan¹ mercy for to crye,   ¹ began
> And spak¹ so faire, and profred him so
>   faste,   ¹ spoke
> That she hir love hym graunted atte laste,
> And swoor hir ooth, by seint Thomas of
>   Kent,
> That she wol been at his commandement,
> Whan that she may hir leyser¹ wel espie.   ¹ opportunity
>   (I. 3288–93)

The lover's appeal and the lady's acquiescence are interspersed with the homely oath by a popular saint and
pragmatic questions of time and place, and the process of
love-service is enacted in a matter of minutes.

For the Knight's broad historical vision the Miller
substitutes a world where time is measured only by the in-
finitely renewable cycles of day and week, and Providence is
reduced to the granting of sexual pleasure. His "first mover"
is Nicholas, whose male designs take shape, not in a "fair
chain of love," but in a chain of circumstance, a material

economy so self-consistent and complex as to seem virtually organic. As Theseus creates his great theater, the monument to a chivalry which emulates the beneficent hierarchical order of the universe, so Old John, the credulous husband, is prompted by Nicholas to capitalize on "Goddes pryvetee," and build the elaborate machinery which effects the climax of the tale.

Chivalry ennobles what are too often only the confused workings of male desire. The conventional Christianity which is the ruling ideology of the Miller's Oxenford, its counterpart to Theseus' chivalric world view, exists only to be exploited in the service of that same desire. Nicholas' clerical skills, his eloquence and Biblical lore impose his authority on old John, whose simple faith is readily persuaded that he and Alisoun are exempted from the effect of the prophesied flood. Elsewhere religion becomes the emblem of desire. Nicholas' song of the angel's salute to Mary announces his abrupt physical address to Alisoun, and their lovemaking is carried on until the hour of Lauds, when its joys are summed up by a Friars' chorus chanting the divine goodness. Even Absolon's unfortunate kiss is preceded by a love-song, charged with echoes of the Song of Songs and thus evoking the kiss with which the Song begins, traditionally a symbol of the love that links God to each human soul.

But the tale is also about the abuse of innocence. In fleshing out his fabliau material, Chaucer endows John, the traditional cuckold husband, with attributes that complicate our response to his plight. He is devout and industrious as well as foolish, and though his religion is mostly credulity, he is also humane. His concern over Nicholas' seeming illness is genuine, and he responds to the thought of Alisoun's drowning with a horror in which uxoriousness mingles with selfless devotion. But his finest qualities are precisely those which reduce him to Nicholas' puppet. The community at large abounds in a similarly innocent and vulnerable good will. We see it in the chatty solicitude with which the monk of Oseneye draws Absolon aside to discuss the possible whereabouts of old John, and in the banter of Gervays the smith as he unwittingly provides Absolon with the means to his revenge. Nicholas himself is sufficiently detached from the prevailing atmosphere to be able to imitate it, as in his charming but cynical conjuring-up of the aftermath of the flood:

> Thanne wol I clepe,[1] 'How, Alison! how,
>   John!   [1] call
> Be myrie,[1] for the flood wol passe anon.'[2]   [1] merry [2] soon
> And thou wolt seyn,[1] 'Hayl, maister
>   Nicholay!   [1] say
> Good morwe,[1] I se thee wel, for it is day!'   [1] morrow
>   (I.3577–80)

"Maister" is an important word here, a mark of the clerical authority on which Nicholas' power depends. Though the trappings and avocations of his Oxford life are precisely contrasted with those of the austere pilgrim Clerk, he is viewed as a clerk within the world of the tale, and his control of that world is a comment on the power of the educated cleric for good or ill. It is the worldliness of both clerks in the story, and their conflict over a worldly matter, that leads to the tale's violent conclusion. Like the Knight's unwieldy chivalry, the tainted clerical values of the Miller's tale generate division and violence under the guise of an enlightened order. And here, too, the proliferation of division ends by involving all the principals in accident and unforeseen reciprocity, revealing their ultimate lack of freedom. Both clerks are punished in a manner befitting their pretensions, and even Alisoun, though she escapes scot-free from the chain of just reprisals that resolves the plot, is equally a victim of her circumstances. Released from her elderly husband's "cage," she is only subjected to new constraint. When she struggles like a colt in Nicholas' arms, the image of youthful energy foretells her submission to the hand that holds her in check.

There is, moreover, a strong hint of sexual violence in Absolon's "quiting" of his unfortunate kiss. Bitter in his disillusionment with love, he plies his sizzling coulter indiscriminately, and has no way of knowing that it is Nicholas rather than Alisoun that he wounds. The smithy where the genial Gervays plies his trade is an outpost of the temple of

Mars. But if the story ends by exposing its self-renewing, comic-strip world as an illusion, it is only Old John whose misfortune is emphasized. His broken arm is a discord amid the general hilarity, and it is clerks who set the tone of the merriment at his discomfiture, collaborating in Nicholas' protestation that John is simply mad, and making us suddenly aware of social division. But the miller remains detached, and offers no final reflection on the potentially anarchic implications of his comic creation.

In the Reeve's Cambridge the innocent community of the Miller's Oxford is replaced by an economy that binds people together in spite of themselves, generating ambitions and antagonisms that foreclose any hope of happiness. No chivalric idealism or clerical ingenuity shapes the world of this tale. The first mover is the local parson, whose use of parish funds to dower his illegitimate daughter sanctions the social ambition of the miller Symkyn, creating the tensions necessary to the plot of the story.

Probably a peasant by birth, the Reeve can speak with authority about competition and upward mobility, but there is no sign that his experience has enriched him. For all his economic success, he is obsessed by the inevitable waning of his vitality with age. His prologue, largely a meditation on the paradoxical inherence of lust in an organism that lacks the physical substance to sustain it, culminates in a single, terrible image of life as a constant dwindling towards dotage and death:

> For sikerly,[1] when I was bore,[2] anon 　　　　[1] surely [2] born
> Deeth drough[1] the tappe of lyf and leet it 　　　　[1] drew
> 　　　　　　　　　　gon;
> And ever sithe[1] hath so the tappe yronne[2] 　　[1] since [2] run
> Til that almoost al empty is the tonne.[1] 　　　　[1] barrel
> The streem of lyf now droppeth on the
> 　　　　　　　　　chymbe.[1] 　　　　[1] rim
> 　　　　　(I.3891–95)

There is a homiletic undertone in the Reeve's words which reverberates like a distant bell, but the force of his sententiousness is wholly negative. It expresses, not *contemptus mundi*, but contempt for self, and for all who expect anything but disappointment from life.

This bitterness comes to bear on Symkyn, whose every success takes the form of an assertion of status. His abuse of his "sokene," a monopoly on milling which entitled him to exact a toll, imitates the Parson's abuse of the authority and resources of the Church, and his family connections are what he most values. But his wife's high birth and nurture bear the taint of illegitimacy, and despite his high hopes for his daughter, her squat figure and simian physiognomy expose her lowly origins. The baby who completes the menage is "a proper page," but in such a world the very existence of an infant so much younger than his putative sister is sufficient to suggest that she may already have been "disparaged" before her encounter with the clerk Aleyn in the tale.

The narrowness of this world is stressed in many ways. At the outset Symkyn untethers the clerks' horse, and its "wehee" as it gallops off in quest of "wilde mares" expresses a freedom none of the human characters enjoy. Symkyn's "sokene" includes the university, but the clerks bring no larger dimension of learning or imagination into his world, and act in full conformity with his exploitative notion of human relations. Even their sexual escapades are a form of revenge. By the end, after the confused shifting of beds in the dark chamber and the final chaotic struggle, an image of society fittingly compared to the state of "pigges in a poke," the social structure defined by the Parson's legacy and Symkyn's ambition has collapsed. The clerks return to a world outside the story, leaving Symkyn and his family humiliated and diminished.

A moment that expresses the moral poverty of the tale is the parting of the clerk Aleyn from the miller's daughter after their night of love-making. In the best tradition of courtliness, the lovers' farewells form an aubade or dawn-song, affirming their love as day forces them to part. The exchange of pledges is oddly augmented by Malyn's added gift of information as to where her father has hidden the cake made from the clerks' stolen flour, but she ends on what seems like a note of real feeling, almost weeping as she commends her lover to God's care. A moment later Aleyn, creeping into what he thinks is the bed of his fellow-clerk, belies his own sincerity: his gloating report of his sexual conquest instantly triggers the violent indignation of Symkyn and battle ensues. Like the resonant assertion of Malyn's high "lynage" (birth), which punctuates Symkyn's horror at the violation of all he holds dearest, the courtly exchange is at odds with its context. Whatever sincerity we impute to Malyn's words, their incongruity expresses the Reeve's bitter skepticism about the efficacy of love. The last word on the tale is the Cook's. It is a "jape of malice in the dark," a study of meanness inspired by meanness, and perhaps most telling as a comment on its narrator, who has risen socially to the point of learning to despise his own craftsmanly origins, but without gaining access to any larger world.

The Cook's own tale of Perkin the Reveller takes us beyond the pale. Perkin has the youth and vitality of a Nicholas, but his energy is that of a little bird or animal: elusive, lustful, and incapable of moral reflection. When he is dismissed from his apprenticeship and removes to the house of a friend whose wife, behind a respectable shop-front, earns her living as a prostitute, we reach a level at which social forms are at the mercy of the basest appetites, and here Chaucer was clearly content to break off.

The sort of *ad hominem* conflict that generates the Reeve's attack on the Miller reappears in the opposition of the Friar and Summoner. As competing representatives of religion, one embodying the authority of the established Church at its most corrupt, the other offering an alternative to that authority, the two are natural enemies. The Friar, a professional preacher, attacks the Summoner through a traditional exemplary story with a clear moral, while the Summoner, though he draws on traditional satire against the fraternal orders, ends with a coarse scatological joke worthy of the Cook. But the Summoner's tale is in fact far more effective satire than the Friar's, richer and more humane in its very grossness than the other's cold authoritarianism. The

degenerative tendency of the opening fragment is here checked
by a lowest-common-denominator humanity that mitigates
harsh criticism with humor and good will.

   In the Friar's tale a summoner, having fallen in with a devil
disguised as a bailiff, unwittingly damns himself by provoking the sincere curse of a good woman whom he attempts to
bribe. The tale is an efficient vehicle, and the Friar uses it
well, but much in the story seems strangely at odds with his
purpose. His summoner is not a good man — the story's
point is to show him more rapacious and less fair-minded
than the devil himself — but he is a very human and lonely
one, and it is this that makes him claim the devil as his friend.
The word "brother" occurs some twenty times in this short
tale, and the summoner shows a dog-like fidelity in preserving
the illusion of brotherhood with one who seeks only to
possess his soul:

> For though thou were the devel Sathanas,
> My trouthe[1] wol I holde[2] to my brother,   [1] promise [2] keep
> As I am sworn, and ech of us til[1] oother,   [1] to
> For to be trewe brother in this cas . . .
>   (III.1525–28)

Though the fiend is open about his true nature, the summoner
persists in the view that they are fellow yeomen and professionals, between whom honor and intimacy are possible and
fitting.

   The Friar seems blind to the human side of his creation.
Throughout he assumes that his summoner is motivated
solely by greed, and at times he seems not even to catch the
tone of his speech:

> This somonour, which that was as ful of
>   jangles,[1]   [1] chattering
> As ful of venym been thise waryangles,[1]   [1] shrikes
> And evere enqueryng upon every thyng,
> "Brother," quod[1] he, "where is now youre
>   dwellyng   [1] said
> Another day if that I sholde yow seche?"[1]   [1] seek
>   (III.1407–11)

Far from idle chatter or venom, the summoner's question is

guileless, even wistful, and wholly out of keeping with the Friar's description of it.

The source of the summoner's incongruous human appeal is his model, the Summoner of the General Prologue, a loathsome predator but a man of pathetic needs and longings. The pilgrim Summoner's abuse of his office is largely motivated by a desire to share the lives of others, born of a loneliness so deep as to make him enter willingly into fellowship with the equally alien and unappealing Pardoner. A man whose incurably diseased face terrifies children might well feel the fascination that makes the summoner in the tale ask again and again about the fiend's power to change his appearance at will, and the two are equally reckless of the spiritual meaning of their abuse of office: the fate of the Friar's summoner fulfills the ominous reminder in the pilgrim Summoner's portrait that "curse will slay."

As the two summoners resemble one another, so the Friar resembles the fiend who enacts his vicarious condemnation, a two-dimensional figure, repellent in the bland ease with which he exploits the summoner's weakness. It is he who first proffers friendship, and draws the other remorselessly forward with "soft" and confiding words. Even at the last, he can preface the announcement of the summoner's damnation with the unctuous mock-commiseration of "Now, brother, be nat wrooth . . ." The illusory sympathy and total detachment recall the Friar's own cynical traffic in absolution as described in the General Prologue.

An astute professional like the Friar could not fail to exploit so glaring a weakness as the Summoner's loneliness; as he himself remarks, a good hunting dog can tell a hurt deer from a healthy one. This is said of the summoner in the tale, but he in fact does himself in by pursuing an all too healthy deer in the person of the doughty old woman who finally damns him, and the remark applies far better to the Friar himself. The Friar's tale serves not so much to expose the sinfulness of its protagonist − though that is not spared − as to dramatize the unredeemed coldheartedness of its teller, who can remorselessly exploit the most vulnerable aspect of a fellow human being in order to damn him.

The Summoner's tale consists almost entirely of the self-display of a friar whose relentlessness in soliciting money from a sick man provokes a gross and humiliating reaction. The tale is if possible even more singleminded than the Friar's, but the figure under attack is unredeemed by any mitigating trace of weakness or need. "Friar John" is a brilliant comedian whose professions of concern, as friend and confessor, have a shameless, Falstaffian charm, but clearly express his utter, unreflecting hypocrisy. The Summoner controls our response by focusing on the externals of the friar's behavior. The friar's own words make up two-thirds of the tale, giving him ample opportunity to "glose" his conduct and reducing him to the sum of his own false posturings. What is condemned is less a human being than a personification of hypocrisy and false authority.

Friar John himself insists repeatedly on his virtual im-materiality as one not subject to normal human needs. A friar, he says, draws his nourishment from the Bible that "fosters" his spirit, but his relation even to biblical sustenance is chiefly a matter of the abuse of his authority to interpret it. "Glosing" is the essence of the friar's hypocrisy: his ostentatious preferring of spiritual meanings to mere literal things is so much a part of his all-purpose rhetoric that he has lost sight of its implications. His insistence on the abstinent poverty that guarantees the efficacy of friars' prayers is flatly contradicted by his appeals for money, but he harps on these pet themes in complacent unawareness of the incongruity, and as he lectures Thomas on the sin of wrath he is wholly oblivious to the wrath he is generating in his all-too-human listener.

The fart with which Thomas rewards his would-be confessor is a fit rejoinder to his spurious assertion of authority. Friar John had prepared us for it with his own memorable image of the friars' arch-enemy, the fat and well-fed benefice-holder, belching while reciting his office and "glosing" his indelicacy with the Psalmist's "My heart has uttered [lit. 'belched forth'] a good word." The idea of "spirituality" as flatulence, a by-product of overindulgence rather than an act of piety, is a comment on the effect of the friar's own preaching: like Milton's "hungry sheep" in the grip of a corrupt Anglican clergy, his 'hearers are "swollen with wind," and farting aptly expresses the effect of a surfeit of such discourse.

The fart itself would make a fit ending, but Thomas adds the proviso that it be divided equally among the brothers of Friar John's house, driving the friar to carry the affair, and his humiliation, a step further. Enraged, he seeks redress from the lord of the manor, who bids him forget the whole affair. The lord's refusal to take the matter seriously is again an effective last word. But the Summoner adds a coda in which the lord's squire proposes an elaborate method for dividing the fart, centering on a vivid, unmistakable image of the mission of the friars as a parody of that placed upon the Apostles at Pentecost. The excesses of the fraternal orders are thus dismissed as bearing no functional relation to the life of the body of the Church. A tale which had been prefaced by the image of friars swarming like bees around the devil's "ers" ends with Friar John and his brothers enveloped in the flatus of their own false authority.

In the wake of such a conclusion it may seem perverse to argue that the Summoner, for all his unpleasantness, is to be viewed as healthier in his imaginative life than the Friar, but this, I think, is one of the main points of Chaucer's pairing of the two. The Friar's tale is infected by his own inhumanity: his pathetic summoner exists only to be damned. The old woman of the tale is a mere means to this end, and it is a measure of the Friar's unconcern with real justice that once having played her role she is abandoned in her abused and outraged innocence, still (as she recognizes) at the mercy of any charge the Archdeacon's court may propound. In the Summoner's tale, community reasserts itself with a humor like that of the Miller. Indeed the Summoner's tale can be seen as in some sense balancing the Miller's story of the abuse of innocence by showing the several ranks of society acting in concert to repudiate friarly pretension. Its satire is crude, and it offers no final antidote to the power of false apostles, but its resolution (in an atmosphere where unfortunate word-play is hard to avoid) can be said to be purgative. It is a measure of the intricacy of Chaucerian characterization that the tale of this unlovely and tormented character should portray the triumph of instinctual good will.

The Shipman's tale shows instinct at the mercy of the commercial spirit. It defines the relations of its characters in the terms of fabliau, but unlike the Miller's and Reeve's tales, its story of false friendship and cuckoldry seems to run its course at no emotional cost. The principals, a merchant, his wife, and the monk Daun John, share a fondness for good living, and their relations are seemingly governed by the law of fair exchange. The merchant's money enables him to count on a dutiful wife, an orderly household and convivial company; his good will is exploited, but the result seems only to confirm the self-regulating character of his world. A hundred marks pass from him to Daun John as between loving "cousins," and from Daun John to the wife in return for her sexual favors. The wife uses them to buy clothes, in order (as she points out) to do credit to her husband, and then completes the circle by offering her husband sexual gratification as earnest of payment of her ongoing "debt." All these transactions occur, as we are frequently reminded, in private, and at the end the world goes on as before.

On closer examination, however, the economy of the tale is not closed. The relations of the three principals to the sources of their common weal are very different, and there is a clear hierarchy of pleasure and autonomy among them. Daun John's role has a solid institutional basis. Licensed by his abbot to travel, he comes and goes at will. His "courtesy" is as much a commodity as the merchant's wealth or the wife's beauty, but his gifts and tips seem to flow naturally, like the furnishings of the Franklin's table. His well-being is as far removed from the "hap and fortune" of commerce as his "courteous" deployment of his breviary from true soul-searching. His every act is a form of sophisticated play, and he is unique among Chaucer's fabliau seducers in achieving his end at no definable cost.

The wife, too, receives ample gratification, financial and sexual, and the story begins and ends by emphasizing feminine astuteness. But the wife's only resources are her beauty and her function in the merchant's domestic economy. Her freedom to negotiate her position is extremely limited, and she possesses nothing outright. Her clothes, as she points out, set off the merchant as much as herself, and even her sexual pleasure is contingent on the promise of pleasure she offers. As her fencing with her newly ardent husband at the end of the story shows, her success depends on sexual politics.

The merchant's situation is complex. He lives by his own strange standards, in an aura of something like innocence. The plot against himself which his loan initiates is further assisted by his withdrawal from the center of the action into a mysterious private world which the Shipman describes in quasi-devotional terms. The merchant's counting-house is the real center of his life, its *sanctum sanctorum*. He himself can convey its mysteries only in cryptic phrases, and with the portentous suggestion that the true reality of a chapman's life is incommunicable:

> We may wel make chiere[1] and good visage,
>
> And dryve forth[1] the world as it may be,
> And kepen oure estaat[1] in pryvetee,[2]
>
> Til we be deed[1] . . .

[1] outward cheerfulness
[1] move along
[1] state of affairs
[2] secrecy
[1] dead

(VII.230–33)

Commercial considerations mediate every aspect of the merchant's life. His wife is important chiefly as a regulator and essential component of the "honesty" of his house, the face his life presents to the world, and his vigorous response to her welcome at the end of the story is stimulated as much by his recent success in business as by conjugal affection. He enjoys good company, but the camaraderie of Daun John is largely a bulwark against his anxieties over trade. He himself cannot separate what is personal in their relations from a businessman's desire to preserve an impression of open good will; even his fear of having estranged the monk by seeming to hound him over his debt is shown to be a symptom of his acute sensitivity to the danger of offending a business associate.

The merchant's social relations, scrupulously considerate yet devoid of intimacy, resemble the system of *creaunce* (borrowing on credit) and indirect exchange by which he does business. His stock in trade is never specified, and he works mainly by *chevyssaunce*, borrowing large sums in one currency and repaying them in another after the goods they enable him to buy have been sold. Such transactions require clear rules and much trust; in this sense *creaunce* has in the Shipman's tale a function like that of *gentilesse* in the Franklin's. But *chevyssaunce* also amounts to making money with money, exploiting fluctuating rates of exchange to gain an extra profit. This was regarded as usury, and was in fact illegal, but it was a discreet form of manipulation, readily compatible with the outward dignity a merchant was obliged to maintain, and could even be rationalized as a by-product of normal commerce. As a model for social relations the system of *creaunce* is clearly no substitute for courtesy and *gentilesse*. The commercial rectitude of the Shipman's merchant, like the good will it elicits from his companions, is a fundamentally ambiguous quality.

But the merchant himself is the one most affected by this ambiguity. Beneath his veneer of probity and good will lurks a strong unconscious need for human contact. There is a dependency in his attachment to Daun John that goes beyond pleasure in his diverting company. When the monk claims him as "cousin" he responds with naive delight, "as glad thereof as fowel of day." On returning from Bruges to Paris his first impulse is to go and tell Daun John the state of his still unresolved trading venture, as though to draw assurance of the success of his final "creauncing" from the good will of the solid, worldly monk. His anxiety about debt repeatedly expresses itself as a need to communicate with Daun John, and his release from this constraint leads directly to sexual indulgence, suggesting both the repressive and alienating effect of his commercial life on his sense of himself, and his dependence on the monk as a surrogate and model for gratification. His essential isolation is Chaucer's comment on a commercial world of surfaces where the substance of love, courtesy and benevolence cannot be distinguished from their outward forms.

In the tale of the pilgrim Merchant, the effect of the commercial outlook on sexual love and the forms of courtesy is explored in shockingly literal terms. The elderly January, whose ill-considered marriage is the subject of the tale, is ostensibly a knight, but he is also a projection of the Merchant, who announces himself as having made a similarly bad choice. In the long celebration of marriage that opens the tale the Merchant's irony and January's dogged optimism find identical expression. Its most idealizing passages are fraught with what we may hear either as the narrator's bitterness or as an anxiety which the willfulness of the protagonist conceals only from himself. Man and wife, being one flesh, must have a single heart and will: hence the speaker extolls the lifelong fidelity, obedience and physical availability of wives, but with an awareness of how these qualities test the durability and stamina of husbands:

> A wyf wol laste, and in thyn hous endure,
> Wel lenger[1] than thee list,[2] paraventure.[3]

[1] longer [2] pleases you [3] perhaps

(IV.1317–18)

The less we know of Abigail, Rebecca or Judith, the easier we feel with the Merchant's choice of them to exemplify wifely "good counsel." And when he urges "Love wel thy wyf, as Crist loved his chirche," it is appropriate to recall that Christ's relation to the Church is vicarious.

In January male authority is reduced to a sheer denial of reality. He simply assumes that the woman he chooses will automatically comply with his desires, and his pornographic dream is of a "fair shape" as pliable as an image of warm wax. The account of his wedding day tells us more than we want to know about his situation. Amid a hectic atmosphere of loud music and heavy drinking, while Venus, dancing and laughing, moves with demoniacal energy among the throng,

May is a vague presence, a figure of "fairy" whom January
beholds "in a trance." As his mind dwells with grotesque hyper-
bole on the keen ardor with which he must soon assail her, his
underlying fear of physical impotence is tellingly conveyed. But
the crisis must finally be faced, and in the event we are spared
almost nothing. We see January virtually embalm himself with
aphrodisiacs, and we observe his prolonged foreplay, most of it
verbal and consisting largely of elaborations on the maxim that
one cannot work both well and hastily. After an interval of
undefined "labour" he drinks, sings loudly, plays and chatters
in a wanton way, and eventually falls asleep.

The painful inevitability of this impasse is not January's
only problem. Already at the wedding feast Venus' torch had
aroused his squire Damyan to a passion for May. Henceforth
the main concern will be the interaction of this relationship
with that of May and January. In the interval of awkward
stasis following the wedding-night, the Merchant summons
Damyan into the story again in a curiously deliberate way:

> *Now wol I speke* of woful Damyan,
> That langwissheth for love, *as ye shul[1]*
>   *heere*;   [1] shall
> *Therfore I speke to hym* in this manere:
> *I seye*, "O sely[1] Damyan, allas!   [1] wretched, poor
> *Andswere[1] to my demaunde*. . .   [1] answer

(IV.1866–72)

The gist of this passage could be conveyed by a mere phrase
("And what of Damyan?"). The Merchant's elaboration tells
us that Damyan is *needed* at this point in the story: his passion gives the plot a new lease on life, and he plays a similar
role in the lives of both May and January. When husband and
wife reappear together after May's post-nuptial retreat,
January's first thought is of the ailing squire. He dwells at
length on Damyan's virtues; resolves to visit him directly in
company with May; then decides to send May but defer his
own visit in favor of an interval of rest; May is to join him
on her return from the sick-bed.

It is as if January's own sexual confidence were somehow
renewed by thoughts of his "manly" and "serviceable"

squire, as he had earlier been brought to the threshold of consummation by a sheer willed imagining of potency. But it is the perverse, Midas-like nature of his sexual imagination that its desires are invariably confounded by material obstacles. His vicarious identification with Damyan leads to new sexual failure, and only serves to quicken May's awareness of the flesh-and-blood squire. January plunges further into fantasy, a retreat which will end by excluding the everyday world so utterly that sex itself, when it surfaces at last in a natural form, will have the effect of nightmare.

It is only now that we first learn of January's garden, a private paradise to which he alone possesses the key, and where, we are told, he performs things that cannot be accomplished in bed. The garden climaxes his laborious imagining of a world of perfect unreality, and it is fitting that in bringing his fantasy to this consummation he creates the means of his own real-life betrayal, setting the stage for a fabliau conclusion which will expose him once and for all as that standard butt of satire, the elderly and deluded cuckold.

The turning-point, the moment at which January's rejection of reality begins to generate an equal and opposite reaction, is marked by his being suddenly struck blind. Simultaneously he is assailed for the first time by jealousy, and from this point his power of self-delusion steadily declines. His loss of autonomy is indicated by the ease with which May and Damyan infiltrate the garden, and his very imagination becomes subject to May's control. It is her "egging," rather than a spontaneous impulse, that draws him into the garden on the day of his betrayal: the parody of the *Song of Songs* with which he "summons" her is his highest flight of sexual fancy, an assertion of desire made doubly pathetic by the blatant religious echo in "No spot of thee ne knew I al my lif," one more hint that for all January's efforts May remains technically "immaculate." But rather than heralding yet another desperate attempt to perform sexually, the song introduces a sober speech, tainted by the offer of a bribe and a disingenuous review of January's original motives for marriage, but frank and even touching in acknowledging his dependency on May's fidelity. May and the Merchant show no sympathy. May's effortlessly cynical conduct is ample reward for the sin of having viewed love as essentially a commercial transaction, an exchange of goods and services in the interest of self-gratification.

The Merchant's bitter contempt extends to the ideals themselves which January exploits. In this tale the opposition between the abstractive tendency of courtly romance and the sexual realism of the fabliau is expressed in the workings of a single male psyche. When May and Damyan act out their fabliau intrigue, they do so at the very center of a garden that is the archetypal setting of the courtly love-vision. In exposing the artifice that sustains this vision, they suggest a sense in which the courtly ideal itself is no more than a self-protective male fantasy, a sublimation of the feminine that conceals a deep fear of active feminine sexuality. The pear-tree episode, the vehicle of the story's fabliau plot, brings this fear to the surface. The basic story exists in many versions, but it is normally two male figures, commonly God and St. Peter, who observe the situation, restore the husband's sight at the crucial moment, and end by acknowledging the incorrigibility and astuteness of woman. The introduction of a female goddess, Proserpine, to collaborate in May's cuckolding of January is Chaucer's own contribution, and gives a peculiar sanction to May's conduct: as Proserpine's own role as fertility goddess depends on her separating herself from her husband for a season each ycar, so May (who has already hinted strongly, in the face of the story's every insinuation, that she is somehow pregnant by January) may grow fertile in the arms of Damyan. Infidelity is elevated to the status of a cosmic principle. Feminine duplicity, rather than male providential authority, now ensures the continuity of life.

At the sight of the intercourse of Damyan and May January expresses his sense of shock by crying out, "As dooth the mooder whan the child shal dye." He is emerging from fantasy for the first time, and the powerful comparison expresses the shattering of a delusion that had been more real and precious than life itself. But he is also fascinated: while the Merchant in narrating the sexual event frames the memorable verb "throng" (thrust) in leering euphemisms, January insists directly and repeatedly on the concrete fact. Though he is gradually persuaded to accept it as a lingering effect of his blindness, we last see him, evidently aroused by what he had thought he saw, and "glad" for perhaps the first time in the story, busily kissing and caressing May as he leads her home.

But January is also concerned in his own way with the question of literal progeny. May's hints at pregnancy may have revived it in his mind, and it is suggested again by the tenderness with which he strokes her womb in the final lines. At the beginning of the tale January had expressed his desire for an heir with painful vividness:

> Yet were me levere[1] houndes had me eten,   [1] I would prefer
> Than that myn heritage sholde falle
> In straunge hand . . .
>
> (IV.1438–40)

But the powerful imagery here is potentially misleading. January's desire for children, like all aspects of his wedded life, is divorced from natural process. His real concern is what will become of his wealth. This inert, characterless extension of himself is the "heritage" of the lines just quoted. Wealth has fueled his sexual ambitions, and it is by bestowing on May "al myn heritage" that he seeks to retain her love after his failure as a sexual partner has become undeniable. His gladness at the conclusion of the poem may express a recognition that with the promise of this heritage and the help of Damyan he can retain and in his own way enjoy May. Her "freshness" may yet come to fruition in the production of a child who, endowed with his name and substance, may be a monument to himself. Such a bargain would carry vicarious sexual experience one last stage further, reducing January to the sponsor of a procreative act, and so ratifying his own total alienation from natural sexuality. January is incorrigibly the pornographic hero, all too grotesquely real, yet totally isolated in an artificial environment of fantasy brought to material realization by wealth. For Chaucer his dilemma represents the final barrenness of a life founded on acquisition.

The Pardoner is in many ways the most representative of the churls, a man openly and avowedly committed to acquisition, yet one whose rapacity and cynicism mask a deep longing for love and fellowship, and a bitter hatred of his condition. A professed materialist, savage in his scorn for those who are moved by his brilliant preaching to place their trust in his powers of absolution, he is also in certain respects the most spiritually alive of the pilgrims, and his worldly and religious selves are in conflict. He insists, repeatedly and defiantly, on his indifference to the spiritual implications of what he does, but he is obsessed with the paradox of being uniquely immune to the effects of his own eloquence, and fearful that his abuse of his office, his incorrigible depravity and, most of all, his physical sterility, are a kind of curse, the signs of an incurable spiritual sickness.

But the Pardoner is also justly proud of the preaching that earns him his living, and even takes a certain pride in his official authority as an agent of the Church − an authority not necessarily invalidated by his flagrant abuse of his office, and which Chaucer never denies. Emboldened by these, he uses his alien status among the pilgrims to his advantage, exploiting their uneasiness to control their attention, and even challenging their expectations by laying claim to a normal sexual life in the face of plain evidence of his debility. The magnetic effect of his confession is a way of compensating for his exclusion from ordinary social intercourse.

The bitter side of the Pardoner's social experience is also evident in his performance. He is plainly on guard against personal attack. His credentials serve, he says, "my body to warente" (protect), lest any man "disturb" his performance. He fears to confront those who have done harm to him and his fellow pardoners, but he can "sting" them with the venom of defamation under the veil of denouncing sin. Abuse has evidently been a constant danger, and one of many ironies of his performance is that it ends by provoking a uniquely mortifying threat from Harry Baily. Yet the Pardoner courts hostility. He is obsessed with his sexual abnormality, and unable to view it as a mere accident. Whether he is to be seen as homosexual is not clear, but he resembles homosexuals and victims of racism in more recent times in feeling an obscure responsibility for the condition that sets him apart. Even as he appeals for admiration, his outrageous manner and appearance flaunt the fact of his strangeness, collaborating with the suspicions of others, daring yet simultaneously inviting exposure and punishment. His confession begins as a display of the tricks of the trade, but becomes dominated by an insistence on the selfishness, and above all the impiety of his motives. He makes plain not only that he is greedy, but that his greed is vicious, sinful, a willful violation of holy things. His dramatic skill maintains his hold over his audience, but it is a dangerous game: self-assertion is continually turning into self-exposure, and nothing is fully under his control.

The Pardoner's intense self-absorption is plain in the attack on the so-called "tavern" vices that erupts from him as he begins his tale. A panoramic view of gluttony is followed by briefer condemnations of gambling and the swearing of oaths by the body of Christ. His powerful sensory imagination makes a tour de force of the excess which reduces the body to a privy, where the very processes of digestion become a kind of self-damnation, and he dwells with equal force on drinking, recalling Lot, Herod, and others whose drunkenness led to incest, murder and self-betrayal. Loss of self-possession is the dominant note also in the passage on gambling, and the horror of swearing seems to consist in the contrast between the "idle" nature of the act and the blasphemy it represents. Throughout there is a strong sense of the menace that lurks in relatively innocent pursuits, but in all three cases the threat is disproportionate to the nature of the sin. To indulge the body's need for food is not in itself sinful; gambling does not inevitably lead to "blasphemy, manslaughter, and waste"; and it is hard to see the citing of Christ's blood and bones by Harry Baily or the Miller as a crime worse than homicide.

The true significance of the sermon is not in the nature of the sins condemned but in their importance to the Pardoner himself. It is easy to see in his debasing treatment of gluttony a hostility to the body itself that reflects his own physical problem, and easy, too, to imagine the emotional need that drives him to pursue the very sins he attacks: the lines on cheap wine and drunken sleep have a flophouse authenticity that suggests the sordidness of his way of life. At a deeper level, the harping on excess is that of a man who feels himself betrayed, dragged down to the depths, damned by his own stunted and incorrigible sensuality. He is a sensualist driven to pursue his lusts largely by a distorted awareness of the spiritual implications of what he does, an abuser of sacred duties desperate for some divine indication of disapproval when he willfully exploits his office. The same intense subjectivity is evident in the narrowly focused attack on blasphemy, which centers on the dismembering of Christ in the form of oaths by his blood and body, and gives shape to the deepest and most all-embracing of the Pardoner's obsessions. Just such dismemberments occur at several points in his discourse, and we can hardly gauge the implications for him of this image of absolute blasphemy: identification with Christ's tortured body; recognition that he stands condemned in the light of the sacrament it represents; a consequent fear and hatred of what is nonetheless supremely meaningful to him.

The tale the Pardoner finally tells masterfully develops the confusion in which his three rioters live and move, and we sense that a curse hangs over them as they move haplessly from drunkenness to greed and violent death. But the meaning of the tale is strictly circumscribed, and the rioters themselves remain faceless, creatures of the story's trap-like plot with no trace of the Pardoner's despairing self-consciousness. What renders the tale unforgettable is the apparition of an old man whose role is Chaucer's contribution to the story. In the plot he is a mere signpost, pointing the "crooked way" to the place where Death is to be found, but Chaucer makes him respond to the rioters' questions by describing his life, an endless search for one who will exchange youth for his extreme age. Despairing, and condemned to wander without rest, he longs to die:

And on the ground, which is my moodres[1]
                                    gate,   [1] mother's
I knokke with my staf, bothe erly and late,
And seye 'Leeve[1] mooder, leet me in!   [1] dear
Lo! how I vanysshe, flessh, and blood, and
                                    skyn!
Allas! whan shul[1] my bones been at reste?'   [1] shall
                        (VI.729–33)

There is nothing religious in this yearning, only a desire to be reclaimed by the earth. In the futility of this quest we recognize the Pardoner's own despairing impotence, and the deeper longing that underlies the courting of punishment implicit in his confession, a desire for the oblivion portended by the living death of bodily excess. Recalling his reflections on the "sepulture" of consciousness and responsibility in drunkenness, and the vision of cooks transforming substance to accident, we may now hear in them something of the longing of Marlowe's Faustus at the eleventh hour for disintegration, an escape from the torment of self-awareness into mere materiality. But as the old man cannot die, so the Pardoner remains a soul in anguish, unable to accept or deny the judgment seemingly implied by his abnormal condition. Both figures are strangely empowered to point the way to what they desire, but impotent to pursue it for themselves.

The Pardoner's personal feelings re-emerge in the complex aftermath to his tale. Having brought the story to its dark conclusion, he inveighs in frenzy against the sins implicated by it, then concludes the mock-sermon by affirming his powers of absolution and appealing to his imagined congregation for offerings. He then breaks off abruptly, and adopts a very different tone to commend the pilgrims to the true source of redemption:

And Jhesu Crist, that is oure soules leche,[1]   [1] physician
So graunte yow his pardoun to receyve,
For that is best; I wol yow nat deceyve.
                        (VI.915–18)

This is surely a significant moment for the Pardoner. Granted the opportunity, doubtless rare in his experience, to speak as

a member of a community, licensed and protected by rules
that apply equally to all, he responds to his enfranchisement
with sincerity. But the sense of community proves impossible
to sustain. He withdraws again behind the mask of the per-
former and, all too characteristically tempting fate, proffers
his relics to Harry Baily, bringing upon himself the vicious
response he dreads in the form of a threat of castration.
Whatever the threat may imply about his physical state or
Harry's appreciation of it, it calls attention to his difference
from the other pilgrims in the plainest possible way. The most
painful thing about this exposure is its inevitability, a result
in which the will of the Pardoner and the deeply rooted
masculine prejudices of the Host have collaborated. This conclusion to the Pardoner's performance, reducing him to
traumatic silence and so rendering him impotent in a new
way, leaves us with the question of just what resolution the
story of such a man could have. The Pardoner seems cut off
from any social function save the power his negative example
and self-denying eloquence may exert in the lives of others.
Like most of Chaucer's churls, the Pardoner leaves us with
a sense of the emptiness of his experience of life, but none of
the others, perhaps no other character in literature, conveys
such a sense of fallenness, and Chaucer suggests no comfort
for his despair.

Chapter 5

Women

The exaltation of women is one of the commonest conventions of medieval poetry. The beloved object of sexual love provides a focus and inspiration for courtly delicacy and chivalric enterprise. The bounty and compassion of a Virgin Mary or Goddess Nature provide a model for social relations, compensating the uncertainties of human order and mitigating the rigor of male authority. But the idealizing of more simply human female figures is often fundamentally exploitative, serving not so much to affirm the inherent value of woman as to dignify the masculine chivalry that exalts it. To be thus exalted is to be isolated from normal human relations, subjected to a standard of purity whose very rigidity expresses the fears that lurk beneath the veneer of reverence. For with the ideal image of woman there coexists the "realistic" view of an irrational creature of whim and appetite, constantly in need of the discipline of superior male judgment. Between these opposing views there is little or no middle ground. The social function of woman is sufficiently defined by male-generated strictures on purity and wifely duty so that no autonomous image of woman exists and "feminism" is inconceivable.

Three of the tales treated in this chapter, those of the Man of Law, Clerk, and Physician, exhibit the idealizing view of woman, exposing with increasing irony the self-serving male motives that inform it. In a fourth, the Wife of Bath, the first of Chaucer's female narrators, assails the tradition that defines women's role so narrowly. Her tale is an answer to the Man of Law and a goad to the Clerk, and in her hands misogynist clichés become vessels of something like a feminist critique of male authority. But it is a measure of the limitation of the Wife's situation that she never attains the point of envisioning an alternative to the stereotypical view, and Chaucer's other female narrators show themselves equally incapable of doing so. In the Prioress we see a woman whose confusion of mind and feeling regarding her religious vocation, her woman's nature, and the world at large place her at the mercy of a crude and pernicious story. But despite the complex emotions to which her tale gives vent, she remains, like the Wife of Bath, incapable of imagining an existence freed from authoritarian social and religious strictures. The Second Nun, whose vocational commitment seems devoid of any taint of personality, offers a gentle and canonical version of the legend of St. Cecilia, in which the theme of marriage and the idealization of woman are finally integrated successfully into a religious tale. But even here limitations are apparent. Cecilia's sainthood entails the obliteration of anything that might identify her with the life of women as the other tales have presented it. Her story is a direct communication of the traditional authority of the Church, and has nothing to say about the problematic status of women in the world.

After the increasing disorder of the first fragment, the Man of Law's tale seems to reaffirm the ultimate benevolence of the universe. It is the story of Custance, daughter of the Emperor of Rome, whose wanderings in a hostile world are overseen by divine Providence and culminate in reunion with her father. The tale is a hagiographic romance, and its hybrid form is important to its intended effect. As a romance of voyage, it depicts a world radically open to fortune, where casting out upon the ocean is an act of faith and resolution can be indefinitely deferred. But the hagiographic aspect of the narrative guarantees ultimate fulfillment: if the historical status of Custance is equivocal, her life expresses history's true meaning: not, as in the Knight's tale, a burdensome reminder of recurring disaster in human affairs, but the record of a divinely sanctioned transcendence of human problems.

But the Man of Law's tale is strangely unaffirmative, and

remains suspended between hagiography and sentimental tragedy. Custance is the missionary Church personified, an embodiment of the threat or promise of radical transformation, and ultimately invulnerable; but for the Man of Law she is also a helpless woman who must be constantly protected from contact with the world, an ikon in a series of tableaux which set off her sorrow and helplessness, and isolate her as far as the plot allows in a never-never land of sentimental piety.

The Man of Law prefaces his tale with an odd literary excursus that recalls Chaucer's many tales of heroines who meet with unhappiness in love. Such stories excite his imagination, and emerge from memory with a new vividness, as in his gratuitous reference to the "woundes wide" of Lucretia or the uncanonical assertion that Medea's children died by hanging. He ends by recalling a story Chaucer has *not* told, that of the incestuous love of King Antiochus for his daughter. The graphic image (apparently his own invention) of Antiochus throwing his daughter to the pavement give the story a lurid force out of proportion to its parenthetical status in his catalogue. It is embellishment of a similar kind that flaws the Man of Law's own tale, reducing a religious allegory to a story that threatens violence towards its heroine while keeping her immune from it.

A striking instance is the scene in which Custance is placed on trial for the murder of Hermyngeld. The Man of Law insists strenuously on the absence of any witness on her behalf:

> An Emperoures doughter stant[1] allone;   [1] stands
> She hath no wight[1] to whom to make hir   [1] person
>   mone.[2]   [2] complaint
> O blood roial, that stondest in this drede,
> Fer[1] been[2] thy freendes at thy grete nede!   [1] far [2] i.e. are
>   (II.655–58)

But this stress on Custance's isolation is hard to reconcile with the report of the trial itself: King Alla takes seriously the strong popular sentiment on Custance's behalf, and is already strongly disposed in her favor before a confirming miracle occurs. When his scrupulous and humane conduct of the trial is set against the image of Custance as a lamb being led to slaughter, it is as if we were hearing two separate stories. The strange blending of an apparently self-deceiving pietism with a manipulation of his heroine that at times approaches the pornographic reveals a man deeply divided in his attitude toward life and religion. Like the impeccable credentials that have empowered him to use the law as a vehicle for "purchasyng" (gaining title to land), the ostensibly evangelical purpose of the Man of Law's hagiographic narrative veils a deep personal involvement with the story that amounts to a kind of incest.

In this respect we may compare the story of Custance with one which deliberately mocks the sort of melodramatic pathos that corrupts the Man of Law's religious purpose: the tale of the Babylonian princess Alatiel in Boccaccio's *Decameron*. Shipwrecked while on her way to marry the king of Algarve, Alatiel passes through the hands of nine different men before being restored to her father. In the interval, like Custance, she is cut off from her own culture. Her initial seduction is brought about by drink, of which (living under Islamic law) she had had no previous experience, and often a barrier of language hinders communication with her lovers. Like Custance, she is a cause of violence in others, but remains immune to its effects. As Custance emerges tearful but unscathed from her bloody Syrian wedding feast, so Alatiel survives the moment in which the Duke of Athens, having just assassinated a previous lover, throws himself upon her naked body while his hands are still covered with blood. In the total absence of cultural norms her sexual attractiveness assumes a magical power of protection and mediation very similar to that of the pathos-inducing piety of Custance. And as Custance in the end "escapes" her worldly experience to the haven of Rome, so Alatiel is restored, safe and sound, to her father, who marries her to her originally intended husband as if she were still a virgin. In both tales the exclusion of social and cultural reality allows fantasy to assume an extraordinary dominance. Alatiel's story is a fantasy of innocent promiscuity, charming in its implausibility and finally

innocuous. The Man of Law's tale is a disguised fantasy of incest, and the "providential" design that brings her inexorably
home to her father in the end, like the manipulation of sentiment that heightens the pathos of her situation, shows an
authoritarian view of life being undermined from within. The
element of bad faith in the Man of Law's treatment of
Custance will recur in other of Chaucer's narratives of saintly
women.

In a brief epilogue to the Man of Law's tale, another
pilgrim intrudes to declare "My joly [pretty, merry] body
schal a tale telle." No manuscript assigns this line to the Wife
of Bath, but this was probably Chaucer's final intention. The
tone is hers; there is strong manuscript authority for placing
her tale after the Man of Law's; and there is no pilgrim whose
"joly body" could so aptly be linked to the project of tale-
telling, or provide a sharper contrast to the ghost-like
Custance. The Wife's autobiographical prologue is largely a
history of her body – its marketability, its desires, its
aging, and the effect of its vicissitudes on her sense of self.
Above all it is the history of that part of her body which,
whether rationalized as her "instrument," "glosed" as her
bele chose, or accorded mythic status as the mark of Mars,
has largely determined her relations with men.

The stated theme of the prologue is "the woe that is in marriage," but at the outset marriage is seen as a source of
power. The Wife repudiates virgin purity as a standard of
female value, and presents herself as a kind of nature-figure,
an embodiment of fecund sexuality. She then shifts abruptly
to the stock role of shrewish and conniving wife; is led to
acknowledge the rejection and dependency that have bedevill-
ed her later years; but ends by describing her victory over a
truly worthy antagonist, her fifth husband, a young clerk
whose main weapon in their battle for sovereignty is an exhaustive knowledge of ancient, patristic, and medieval
teachings on the inferior and reprobate status of women.

The Wife's skill with male weapons like preaching, biblical
exegesis, and misogynist satire is uncanny, but reveals at the
same time how far her role-playing is constrained by rules and

categories established by men. The mock-sermon on pro-
creation that begins her prologue discovers a measure of
freedom within St. Paul's strictures on women, and offers
ingenious literal readings of biblical images which commentators had allegorized as arguments that virginity and holy
widowhood are the only proper roles for women; but con-
founding the exegetes leaves the Wife irrevocably committed
to the sole alternative she knows, the literal, sexual purpose
of marriage. In one sense this is a vocation in itself, but as she
concludes the "sermon" portion of her prologue, her promise
of god-like generosity gives way to a grimly legalistic emphasis on her rights:

> Myn housbond shal it have both eve and
> morwe[1]
> Whan that hym list[1] come forth and paye his
> dette.
>
> (III.149–53)

[1] morrow (i.e. morning)
[1] it pleases him [to]

With the whip-crack of "dette" the Wife is transformed
into the wicked wife of anti-feminist satire, mercenary and
ruthless, and she sustains this one-sided role, recalling her
mockery of the misogynist suspicions of her three "good," old,
rich husbands, for nearly 300 lines. Humor does not exclude
other, franker memories: she tells of feigning sexual pleasure
in return for her old husbands' "ransom," but confesses: "And
yet in bacon hadde I nevere delit" (delight). For all her professed cynicism, success in a marital world where "al is for to
selle" has not been enough, and she ends her imagined
harangue by offering her love on different terms:

> Wy, taak[1] it al! lo, have it every deel![2]
> Peter![1] I shrewe[2] yow, but[3] ye love it weel;
>
> For if I wolde selle my *bele chose*,[1]
> I koude walke as fressh as is a rose;
> But I wol kepe it for youre owene[1] tooth.[2]
>
> (III.445–49)

[1] take [2] bit
[1] by St. Peter
[2] curse [3] unless
[1] "beautiful thing"

[1] own
[2] i.e. pleasure

Here the Wife offers a kind of fidelity in return for appreciation, a thing indefinable in material terms. But even here the

context is one of exchange: the rose-like "freshness" she imagines is not an emblem of courtly exaltation, but the effect of finery obtained through sexual commerce. Placed on the marriage market at the age of twelve, she finds it difficult to value herself in any but economic terms, and when she later recalls her sexual prime, the contrast of her present state, old and unlovely, leads to a bitterly reductive view of commercialized beauty:

> The flour[1] is goon,[2] ther is namoore[3] to telle;   [1] flower/flour [2] gone [3] no more
>
> The bren, as I best kan, now moste[1] I selle.   [1] must
>
> (III.477–78)

Earlier the Wife had dedicated the best of herself, the "flower of her age," to the duties of marriage. Here, by a pun vestigially present in modern English, the "flower" has become "flour" — a commodity in short supply and soon to be replaced by the coarser "bran" of age.

But the Wife can still respond with energy to the memory of earlier days. The clerk Jankyn, her fifth husband, though fully as aggressive as she, had known how to make her enjoy submitting to his will:

> so wel koude he me glose,[1]   [1] i.e. flatter
> Whan that he wolde han[1] my *bele chose*,[2]   [1] have [2] "beautiful thing"
>
> That thogh he hadde me bete on every bon,[1]   [1] bone
> He koude wynne agayn my love anon.
>
> (III.509–12)

Earlier in the Prologue "glosing" had denoted the work of commentators who had made the imagery of the Bible yield a meaning that expressed their own sexual prejudices; here its effect is to make the Wife feel beautiful. Love offered in this context of appreciation is highly desirable, and desire renders her vulnerable. Though she still plays the truant wife of fabliau, she is an aging woman, drawn into a disadvantageous marriage by needs and desires she hardly understands. And once the marriage takes place the atmosphere instantly changes. Jankyn's "glosing" had been the bait in a clerical trap which now springs shut, leaving the Wife in the clutches of a master misogynist whose diversion is to cite endless examples of female wickedness from his "book of wikked wyves." When his insults goad her to violent retaliation, he too emerges from scholarly detachment, and exchanges blow for blow. As in the Reeve's tale, social forms give way to sexual anarchy: in an instant the Wife lies unconscious, and Jankyn is on the point of fleeing, like Perkin from his apprenticeship. Were Jankyn indeed to run away at this moment, the Wife would be truly alone, bereft of youth, beauty, and wealth. But at the very point of losing all, she regains consciousness, coming back to life in a new role as the abandoned heroine of a romance, content to die for love and asking of her betrayer only a final kiss.

Unaccountably, the Wife's revival reduces Jankyn to relieved and grateful submission; he burns his book, restores her property, and grants her full sovereignty within the marriage. She responds with kindness and fidelity, and they live happily ever after. To say that this final episode is too good to be true is to say only that it concludes a highly ambiguous narrative. What has the Wife been seeking, and what has she found? The promise of her imagery of flower and fruit, and her defiant allegiance to the "gentil" text that bids us "wexe and multiplye" have not, apparently, produced children. Even her assertions of hedonism and promiscuity must be weighed against the indignant-sounding claim that though she repaid her fourth husband's infidelities, she did so "nat of my body, in no foul manere"; it may well be that one constraint in her early marriages was her own sense of respectability. The later phase of her life with Jankyn is perhaps the only real happiness she has known, and even if we accept her account of this idyll, we must ask what has happened to him. All that is clear is that success in the commercial aspect of marriage has not been enough. The desire to be valued on less concrete and confining terms, so easily revived by Jankyn's artful glosing, emerges again as a flight of courtly idealism in the tale she tells at long last.

From the outset the tale emphasizes generosity, and

generosity of a peculiarly feminine kind. An Arthurian knight convicted of rape is granted a stay of execution through the intercession of Arthur's queen, who promises him his freedom if he can discover within a year's time what women most desire. Chivalric exploits and conventional legal standards are irrelevant to such a quest; the challenge is to recognize the situation and needs of women. It is a challenge that fascinates the Wife herself. As the knight pursues his quest she comments at length on the suggestions he is given. But her discourse strays. Remarking that all women long to be entrusted with secrets, yet are unable to keep them, she digresses to tell the tale of Midas, whose wife could not hide the secret that her husband had the ears of an ass, and whispered it to the waters of a marsh rather than reveal it to the world.

In Ovid it is Midas' barber who discovers the ears. In the Wife's version Midas' wife not only replaces the barber but becomes the central figure in the story. The secret is her problem, too, and the awkward eagerness with which she rushes to the marsh to "bumble" forth her uncontainable message shows how far her own role is determined by it. The secret stands for the "truth" about marital relations which it is the Wife of Bath's own mission to divulge, and points up a basic problem for both women. In a world controlled by men, women are the brides of Midas, faced with, and inevitably contaminated by, a chronic male blindness to their natures and needs. To tell the truth about men is to reveal their own collaboration in the situation they feel driven to expose; but it is also to reveal the fact that, in the absence of any alternative secular role, their sense of themselves depends on a constant renewal of the antagonism marriage creates.

A way out of the dilemma is suggested by the role of the old, unlovely "wyf" whose wisdom saves the knight and wins him as her husband, and whose restoration to youthful beauty provides a happy ending. In other versions of the story the only role of this "loathly lady" is to vindicate the knight: her intervention attests his essential good character, and her transformation often depends on his demonstrating the

requisite chivalry. In the Wife's version the old wife becomes
the dominant figure, testing and chastising the knight, gaining total control of their relationship, and at last transforming herself, apparently at will. She deals with the knight's lack
of chivalry by delivering a long and frequently beautiful
discourse on *gentilesse*, a speech clearly important to the Wife
of Bath in its emphasis on the inward nature of *gentilesse* and
its availability to all:

> Thanne am I gentil, whan that I bigynne
> To lyven vertuously and weyve[1] synne.   [1] abandon
>
> (III.1175–76)

The idea is an obvious one, but it has a special appeal for a
woman whose career has been an endless flirtation with
disreputability, yet who senses unfulfilled capacities in
herself. The speech as a whole is the most striking of the
several ways in which Chaucer expresses covert sympathy
with the Wife's need to discover her own intrinsic value.

But like the tale of Midas' wife, the gentility speech has no
real function in the plot of the tale, and its irrelevance indicates the limits of the Wife of Bath's power to imagine a
transformation of her condition. The knight is allowed some
astoundingly unchivalrous remarks on his wife's ugliness and
low birth, offers no response to her exhortation, and is never
freed from the stigma of rape. As the fantasy of rejuvenation
and happy marriage flowers at the end of the tale, moreover,
the quest for appreciation implicit in the speech is abandoned.
Transformation does no more than fulfill a transparent fantasy of sexual renewal, and in so doing it simultaneously
places the old wife, now young and lovely, at the service of
a male fantasy inherent in the traditional story. Sovereignty
seems to crown the old woman's self-realization, but it also
releases the knight from all responsibility, rewarding him with
a wife who dominates only to gratify. Success for women is
still defined by marriage, and marriage is defined by male
expectations. It would seem that fourteenth-century insight
into social relations extends no further, and that the Wife and
secular womankind must remain the brides of Midas.

As the Wife frequently reminds us, the chief proponents of traditional misogyny have been clerks. Chaucer's own Clerk may well seem as free of personal animus as the Knight, but his tale of the testing of the patient Griselde by her mysterious and tyrannical husband Walter reveals that he has listened carefully to the Wife's account of her battles, ideological and physical, with the clerical tradition. The tale in its received form is a powerful vindication of male authority, and when the Clerk appends to it a ballad that explicitly contrasts the limitless patience of Griselde with the self-seeking aggression of "the Wife of Bath and all her sect," he seems clearly to give a clerk's answer to the challenge embodied in the Wife.

But the Clerk's is the most difficult of the *Tales*. Like the saga of Custance, it belongs to the problematic category of hagiographic romance, with its inherent potential for arousing contradictory responses; its emotional appeal resists the decorum of allegory, compelling us to look at it in social terms. The Clerk even seems to create tension deliberately, pointing to the entrenched power of male sovereignty and the exploitative treatment of the female subject, and so complicating the interpretation that the tale in its hagiographic dimension seems clearly to invite. And of course the Clerk's tale, like the Merchant's, is about much more than marriage. Unlike January, who seeks to substitute outright possession for the mediation of contract and authority, Walter is scrupulous in eliciting Griselde's agreement to his explicit terms; but when he enters her humble cottage, he brings with him the hereditary power of lord over vassal, and much of the force of the tale is in its depiction of the enigma of such power, necessary yet ever liable to abuse.

The story of Griselde enters literature as the final tale of Boccaccio's *Decameron*, where it concludes a sequence of stories illustrative of the virtue of magnanimity with a negative example of "senseless brutality." The patience of the peasant-girl-turned-queen shows "that celestial spirits may sometimes descend even into the houses of the poor," but the tale chiefly reminds us that some noblemen are no better than swineherds. When Boccaccio's friend and mentor Petrarch read the story, however, he was moved by its grave "sweetness" to produce his own, more formal Latin version, "to move my readers to imitate at least the constancy of the woman, so that what she showed to her husband they might dare to offer to God" (*Epistolae seniles* 17.3). Petrarch's Walter is a true aristocrat, drawn by *noblesse oblige* to submit to the "lawful yoke" of marriage. Curiously, the thralldom he imposes and the unexplained necessity which governs his actions suggest far more than Boccaccio's version the kind of dominance we associate with the "dark lord" of folk-tale. But Petrarch refuses to pass judgment, and by thus mystifying Walter's role renders his behavior more compatible with the prevailing religious decorum.

The Clerk explicitly follows Petrarch's version, but shows himself wary of its authoritarian implications, and makes clear that the basis of the favor Walter enjoys is power. While the Marquis himself, watchful and enigmatic, remains almost invisible behind the veil of his measured speech and such sparing adjectives as "sober," "softe" (mild) and "sad" (serious), the fulsome rhetoric of his loyal subjects and the pale wonder of Griselde convey the drama of his presence. This effect is sustained after the royal marriage by the contrast between Walter's aloofness and the public conduct of his wife. Eloquent, astute in resolving conflict, Griselde is above all *visible*. The people love to "look in her face," coming from far and wide to do so, and she works her wonders even when Walter is absent. But even as she seems an epiphany of divine clemency, she reflects and mediates the authority of Walter; she is an "outward grace" that confirms his prudence in the world's eyes and remains radically subject to his will.

After carefully establishing these roles at the outset, the story traces a gradual reversal of them. As Walter's temptings grow steadily more outrageous, Griselde withdraws behind a façade of emotional detachment that renders her behavior as enigmatic and ominous as his own. In response, Walter's feelings come more plainly into view, and he shows a marked loss of poise. After the god-like force, at once remote and vivid, of his earlier manifestations, he stages as his final trial of

Griselde's patience the announcement that she is to be dismissed in favor of a new wife, as a public display, and abandons his usual sobriety to assail her "ful boistously" (roughly). Griselde, while she never abandons her ikon-like passivity, shows a growing awareness of her situation. At first her outward behavior and her private feelings are indistinguishable: "This will is in my heart," she declares as she gives up her daughter. But she later speaks of free choice ("my will and all my liberty") as something she left at home with her peasant clothing: what constrains her now is the letter of her obligation to Walter, the duty of conforming her will to his in every detail of "word or work." There is even a certain irony in her meticulous conformity to their contract:

> Naught greveth me at al,
> Though that my doughter and my sone be
> slayn, –
> At youre comandement, this is to sayn.[1]   [1] say
> (IV.646–49)

It has been argued that these lines express Griselde's true feelings, but any hint of inhumanity or masochism they might imply is surely refuted when she is reunited with her children. She abandons her impassivity to reveal the fears that had tormented her in their absence; then, overcome with feeling, she faints:

> And in her swough[1] so *sadly*[2] holdeth she   [1] faint [2] firmly
> Hire children two, whan she gan[1] hem[2]   [1] began [2] them
> t'embrace,
> That with greet sleighte[1] and greet diffi-
> cuyltee   [1] skill
> The children from hire arm they gonne
> arace.[1]   [1] tear away
> (IV.1100–3)

The word "sadly" is carefully chosen. Hitherto, in the sense of "sober" or "serious," it has defined the aura surrounding the relations of Walter and Griselde. Griselde's "sad nature" first attracts Walter's notice, and he looks upon her, not wantonly, but "in sad wyse" (manner). He first tempts his wife in order "hir sadnesse for to knowe," and it is her power to endure, "sad and constant as a wall," that brings him at last to relent. But in the lines just quoted Griselde's conscious will is in eclipse, and "sadness" becomes the expression of a depth and intensity of need which the outward "sadness" of the story has threatened to deny. Griselde's sufferings have indeed been "unbearable," as the Clerk will later concede, and after this sudden eruption of involuntary feeling, the story will be irredeemable as a representation of exemplary patience.

The viewpoint of the Clerk himself remains elusive. At first sight his sympathy with Griselde seems plain. A blunt disapproval of Walter's conduct distinguishes his version of the story from Petrarch's; he stresses the pointlessness of Walter's abuses, appeals to married women to share his indignation, and goes so far as to compare Griselde's patience with Job's, seemingly to her advantage. But this seemingly enlightened view coexists with a tacit endorsement of a more authoritarian one. Husbands are bound to "assay" their wives, and some excess is probably inevitable: not just tyrants but "wedded men" in general are deficient in their sense of "mesure." The Clerk's appeal to women centers, moreover, not on the justice of Walter's conduct, but on his carrying it too far, and his remarks on those whose "condicioun" makes them unable to restrain themselves give no hint of how a Walter might be restrained by others. Indeed when he speaks of such people as "bound to the stake" of their obsession, he seems to suggest that they, rather than their victims, are the proper objects of our pity. Even the culminating comparison of Griselde with Job tacitly legitimizes her suffering by granting it the status of a saintly example.

The Clerk encounters a dilemma when he seeks to end the story. It is and is not an exemplary tale, he claims; we cannot imitate Griselde, yet she is a reminder of things that we can do:

This storie is seyd,[1] nat for that wyves sholde	[1] told
Folwen[1] Grisilde as in humylitee,	[1] follow
For it were inportable,[1] though they wolde;	[1] unbearable

But for that every wight,[1] in his degree,[2]

[1] person
[2] rank, status

Sholde be constant in adversitee
As was Grisilde . . .

(IV.1142–47)

How Griselde's "unbearable" humility differs from the constancy we may ask of ourselves is not made clear. Following Petrarch, the Clerk goes on to discover a religious message: God never simply tempts us, and though he allows us to be beaten by the sharp scourges of adversity, the purpose is not to discover our power to endure, for his wisdom knew all our frailty before we were created. But having said what God's purpose is not, the Clerk does not say what it is. Petrarch finds a positive purpose in God's allotment of suffering – "that he may make our frailty plain to us by illustrations readily and intimately known" – but the Clerk says only that God's governance is "for our best." The moral remains incomplete, and as Helen Cooper remarks, God's reasons for "proving" us are all the more inexplicable for the Clerk's attempts to justify them.

But the Clerk's failure may be a truer response than Petrarch's: it suggests that the tale is inherently dangerous, unalterably a tool of the male authoritarianism it dramatizes. We may, like Petrarch, ignore the pathological character of Walter's behavior, and view the intensity of Griselde's suffering as an effect of the tale's "sweetness," the "pitee" it is designed to produce; but if we once admit doubt on these matters, we must ask whether a healthy response to the story is possible. To preserve its exemplary function we must overlook the "inportable" nature of Griselde's experience; to dwell on that suffering is to risk indulging voyeurism in the guise of "pitee," reducing the story to pornographic fantasy. The dilemma is one in which no amount of "sadness" or "courtesy" can help us.

The Clerk forces us to realize all of this for ourselves, and we can never know how deliberately he has undermined his Petrarchan model. The comic ballad that serves him as an epilogue abandons moral reasoning for an anti-moral

addressed to the Wife of Bath and her "sect." Playing on the
inimitability of Griselde, he exhorts women to repudiate
patience and submissiveness, speak and act with total
freedom, and so reduce their husbands to misery. The ballad
can be seen as acknowledging the tension the Clerk's narrative has created, and its reaching out to the Wife of Bath
is perhaps not wholly ironic. The song makes fun of the self-
assertive woman, but in it the Clerk shows himself with ad-
mirable frankness to be as involved in the world of sexual
give-and-take as the Wife herself.

The tales of the Clerk and Man of Law explore the political
and religious dimensions of the idealization of women. The
Physician's tale is a final harsh comment on the self-deceiving
nature of male authority itself. In the twelve-year-old
Virginia, whose death by the hand of her father Virginius
preserves her honor and vindicates Virginius in the face of the
workings of corrupted justice, the appropriation of the
feminine is carried to the point of virtual annihilation. Her
very beauty is a male fantasy, the work of a "Nature" whose
office begins and ends in perfect responsiveness to the will of
the lord she worships:

> *My lord* and I been ful of oon accord,[1]   [1] are in full
>   agreement
> I made hire[1] to the worshipe of *my lord*.   [1] her
>
> (VI.25–26)

From birth Virginia exists to be perfect: her virtues are static,
and all her actions are negative, restraints of appetite and
avoidances of vice. Only the necessity of visiting a temple exposes her to the lustful gaze of the judge Appius, setting in
motion the plot against her honor. She is more a category
than a person until Virginius, commanded on false charges to
give her up, calls her before him and reveals her name for the
first time:

> "Doghter," quod he, "Virginia, by thy
>   name,
> Ther been two wayes, outher[1] deeth or shame,   [1] either
> That thou must suffre . . ."
>
> (VI.213–15)

Virginia's very name, a female complement to Virginius, denies her autonomy. Everything about her is her father's: to him she is "ender of my life," "my last woe" and "my last joy." But it is she, and not he, who must die: "*My* pitous hand moot [must] smyten of [off] *thyn* heed." Thanking God for letting her die a virgin, she disappears, and the moral of the tale wholly ignores her:

Heere may men seen how synne hath his[1] merite,   [1] its
Beth war,[1] for no man woot[2] whom God wol smyte.   [1] beware
                                                       [2] knows

(VI.277–78)

The emptiness of this conclusion is all the more striking in view of the grim "merite" the story accords to virtue. Virginia is a saint, but has no power to convert; her only effect is to arouse desire, and even the love of her father is so possessive as to amount to a kind of incest. Her spiritual inefficacy is underscored when Virginius, viewing her humility, feels his heart "stabbed" by paternal pity, yet refuses to "convert" from his fatal exercise of paternal authority. A "gemme of chastitee" in a world devoid of spiritual values, she is a physical object to be possessed and violated, a vehicle for male self-assertion.

In Chaucer's source, the *Romance of the Rose*, the Virginia story is told in fifty short lines. What makes Chaucer's version so much longer is a host of seemingly pointless digressions. Self-governance is the distinguishing trait of Virginia's character, but the Physician inserts a long address urging parents and governesses to beware of failing in their charge. Similarly intrusive are the lines that climax his description of Virginia's character. So great is the renown of her goodness

That thurgh[1] that land they preised hire   [1] through
                                echone[2]   [2] everyone
That loved vertu, save Envye allone,
That sory is of oother mennes weele,[1]   [1] well being
And glad is of his sorwe[1] and his unheele.[2]   [1] sorrow
                                                    [2] misfortune

(VI.113–16)

The displacement of Virginia by Envy in these climactic lines, and the odd syntactic linkage which places Envy among the lovers of virtue, illustrate an aspect of the tale which we may call its invidiousness. The Physician's narration assumes a world where the betrayal of innocence has always already taken place, where female protectiveness is as liable as male desire to the taint of prurience, and where nobody can respond directly to the appeal of virtue. His very style is invidious: it continually neutralizes the intrinsic value of Virginia's beauty and virtue, and denies the possibility of loving these things for their own sake. At the outset Nature concludes the celebration of her achievement in making Virginia perfect by denying its significance, adding "So do I alle myne othere creatures." From this point forward any ideal meaning that Virginia's uniqueness might have is consistently evaded or suppressed.

Custance and Griselde are queens, wives and mothers as well as saints, and the incestuous or pornographic hints in their stories are only implications of larger narrative structures. But Virginia exists to be a foil to the distorted feelings of others. Virginius kills his daughter "For love and nat for hate," but here these motives come to the same thing, and Harry Baily tells us more than he knows when he remarks that "Hire beautee was hire deth." Like his professional role, the Physician's tale has no symbolic dimension, and the wholly non-dialectical interaction of beauty and desire that determines Virginia's fate is one of Chaucer's strongest comments on the failure of love in human life.

In the Prioress's tale, a woman whose life has been dedicated to an ideal is given a voice of her own. The result is perhaps the most powerful of Chaucer's religious tales, but its power is generated by a tension between the teller's personality and the inherent force of the story she tells. In the Prioress spiritual aspiration and sexual energy coexist with extreme innocence and an utter lack of self-awareness, and her narration mingles mystical grandeur with maudlin sentimentality and violence. Her prologue, rather surprisingly, confirms the pretensions to both piety and courtly culture so deftly mocked in the General Prologue, but its effect is not simple. She begins by identifying herself with the great chorus, encompassing "men of dignity" and babes at the breast, of those who praise God. But her vehicle is the tale of a miracle of the Virgin Mary, and Mary soon becomes the center of her attention. Her praise is informed by rich echoes of French courtly poetry and of the climactic prayer to the Virgin in Dante's *Paradiso*, and at its center is a strikingly sexual vision of the Incarnation:

> O mooder[1] Mayde! O mayde Mooder free!   [1] mother
> O bussh unbrent,[1] brennynge[2] in Moyses   [1] unburnt
>   sighte,   [2] burning
> That ravyshedest doun fro[1] the Deitee,   [1] from
> Thurgh thyn humblesse, the Goost that in
>   th'alighte,[1]   [1] alighted in thee
> Of whos vertu, whan he thyn herte lighte,[1]   [1] made glad?
>   illumined?
> Conceyved was the Fadres[1] sapience . . .   [1] Father's
>   (VII.465–70)

Here and throughout the tale, Mary is "free," unconstrained by virginity yet unsullied by the quasi-sexual union she undergoes, drawing the divine love to herself and wholly possessed by it, while persevering in a state of inviolate humility. The equipoise of the sexual and the mystical in this passage is perfect, and the Dantean praises that follow are an anticlimax.

But the Prioress cannot rest in adoration of Mary, and the prayer as a whole is marked by a growing sense of her own inability to realize the fullness of Mary's virtue. By the end she feels "too weak" to sustain the weight of her theme. From the sonorous opening praise of God and the ecstatic energy of the central stanza the prayer dwindles to the halting, inchoate impulse of a child barely able to speak. It is as if the very uniqueness of Mary, her mystical fecundity and inexhaustible "bountee" were a challenge to the Prioress's sense of her own womanhood and spirituality. The imagery of childhood is common in mystical writing, but the Prioress carries it to an extreme. In her final comparison of herself to a child "of twelf month oold, or lesse" she abandons the Marian vision of the mystics to embrace the Mary of popular cult, and this attenuated piety will dominate the tale, diverting potential religious feeling into pathos, and leaving the Prioress, in the end, unfulfilled and disoriented.

The tale of the "litel clergeon" (schoolboy), like those of Custance and Griselde, tests our tolerance by its very nature. It asks us to venerate a child of seven whose piety consists in the repetition of a hymn whose content he only dimly understands. The Prioress treats his littleness and ignorance with fetishistic devotion, but viewed as hagiography her tale is fundamentally flawed. Like the purity of Virginia, the saintliness of the little clergeon converts nobody, and leads only to his own destruction. The story sets up a standard of absolute evil in the form of the Jews, whose hateful existence is paradoxically subsidized by the governor of the unnamed Asian city, but who remain unalterably cursed, so exclusively a focus of hostile feeling that they are at one point implicitly censured for moving their bowels. For Christians there can be no commerce with such people beyond the "foul usure" for which they exist. The Jews' indignation at being serenaded twice a day with *O Alma* is the work of Satan, and when the violence to which it goads them is answered with greater violence, the Prioress is wholly approving.

But if the Jews are driven to the act of murder which provokes such violent reprisals, the little clergeon is equally at the mercy of larger forces in provoking them. From the moment at which the sweetness of the *Alma redemptoris* pierces his heart he is programmed for destruction. The song dominates his smallness and timidity; in itself it is always "loud," "bold," or "full merry," but "passes through his throat" involuntarily; the act of singing is compulsive ("He kan nat stynte of syngyng"), and it is the obligation to keep singing that holds him suspended on the threshold of death during the story's drawn-out final episode. By the end the song has come to seem virtually a part of his suffering, like his mutilation, and when he is finally allowed to give up the ghost "full softely," what strikes us is the fact of his release into silence.

The Prioress's identification with her child-hero involves

genuine humility, but it is also an act of appropriation as effective as the Man of Law's maneuvering of Custance, or the fatal devotion of Virginius. Her deep investment in his martyrdom is confirmed by the burst of passionate prayer in which she responds to his murder. Set at the center of the tale, it corresponds to the ecstatic vision of the Incarnation at the center of the Prologue and gives vent to comparably strong and personal feeling:

O martir, sowded¹ to virginitee   ¹ united,
                                                   joined

Now maystow¹ syngen, folwynge evere in oon   ¹ may thou
The white Lamb celestial − quod she −
Of which the grete evangelist, Seint John,
In Pathmos wroot, which seith that they been goon
Biforn this Lamb, and synge a song al newe,
That nevere, flesshly, wommen they ne knewe.
                                    (VII.579−85)

The cumbersome citation of John, and the elaborate stress on virginity are at odds with the naive, anti-authoritarian character of the tale. The Prioress's own deep desire is speaking here, intent on the promised reward that vindicates her cloistered life, and the child's innocence is utterly at the mercy of her intense identification with it.

    This tormented piety is complicated by a desperate longing to imitate Mary. The little clergeon, mindlessly repeating his anthem at the Prioress's bidding, is a grotesque, stunted version of the "sapience" that had come to birth in the Virgin's womb. But only Mary can move "freely" between the roles of maid and mother; the Prioress finds no freedom in chastity, and her tale of holy childhood is not imparted in the perfect generosity of Marian *humblesse*. The child is her talisman, her "gemme of chastite," his value too deeply personal to be easily shared with others. And his experience is a measure of her tense, distorted sense of the world at large. His gratuitous fear of being beaten for his devotion to Mary; his casting into a privy; the recurring focus on his wounded throat − all express the Prioress's horror of a "real" world from which she is cut off by the unnatural innocence of her cloistered life.

And for the Prioress there is no release. Having reported the entombment of the clergeon's little body, she ends her narrative with a line which gracefully invites the pilgrims to unite with her in the hope of salvation represented by the child: "There he is now, God leve [grant] us for to meete!" But the Prioress cannot stop here. In a final burst of energy she turns again to the "real" world of violence and horror, recalling the supposed murder of Hugh of Lincoln at the hands of Jews, as if to confirm on the basis of recent history the reality of the evil which haunts her tale, but at the same time exposing with a new and shocking vividness the hostility that is inseparable from her piety.

It is only in the tale of Chaucer's most nearly anonymous pilgrim, the Second Nun, who is nowhere described and never engages in dialogue with the other pilgrims, that the possibility of a truly efficacious religious narrative devoted to a woman is entertained. In her legend of St. Cecilia a woman occupies center stage, and provides a focal point for intense feeling, but there is none of the elaborately dramatized anxiety about her situation that makes for the fantasy of sexual violence present in undertone in the tales of Custance and Griselde. Not only is Cecilie protected by history — her purity and courage were undisputed historical facts of the great age of Christian martyrdom — but she is surrounded by a veritable nimbus of authority. Her very name requires some thirty lines to interpret, and her femininity is as nearly as possible a transparent medium for the expression of truth. Like other young heroines in Chaucer she is "fair," "bright," "clear" and "white," but the Second Nun carefully defines these qualities as symbols of her wisdom, charity and other virtues. Never do they suggest sexual attractiveness. Like the golden robe that hides Cecilie's hair shirt on her wedding day; the "clear" white clothes of the ghostly old man who expounds the faith to Valerian; or the couple's two crowns, snow white and rose red, which sinful eyes cannot behold, the sole function of her beauty is to symbolize an inner, higher reality.

At the same time the story provides reminders of the con-

straints that govern the lives of women in other tales. Cecilie
spends her wedding day praying to God to preserve her chastity, but cannot, it seems, communicate this wish directly to
Valerian. Instead she tells her new husband of the angel who
already possesses her body and will punish any physical address with death. Valerian is remarkably acquiescent, but
demands visible proof that her guardian is "a verray [true]
angel," vowing to slay both Cecilie and her lover if she has
deceived him. In effect her preservation in an inviolate state
depends on the resolution of a conflict between competing
versions of male authority. And at the story's climax, as a
way of explaining why Cecilie is allowed to live on for three
days after her official execution, we are given an oddly prosaic account of the Roman law that forbids an executioner to
strike more than three blows. Secular as well as religious
authority has a determining influence in her earthly life, and
her autonomy and strength are wholly a function of her
assurance of the life beyond – an assurance, we may note,
mediated entirely by men. Even as a religious figure she is
finally little more than an attractive package for truths whose
ratification is provided by the angels and holy men who lurk
in the background. And in the secular world she has no such
talismanic protection as the inviolable constancy of Custance.
The threat posed by her physical attractiveness is
authoritatively suppressed, but as the only woman in a world
of men she remains hardly less physically vulnerable than the
Physician's Virginia. The real difference between her tale and
those of Chaucer's other holy women is the wholly other-
worldly emphasis of the Second Nun's narration, an emphasis
that points forward to the Parson's tale, where narrative and
human drama will give way to a straightforward exposition of
moral and spiritual doctrine.

Chapter 6

The art and problems of tale-telling

The Pilgrims' stunned reaction to the Prioress's tale is conveyed in a brief passage that preserves the rhyme-royal stanza of the tale, as if the Prioress's voice were still reverberating in the air. To such a performance there can be no response, and it is fitting that the pilgrim narrator's own tale of Sir Thopas, which follows, is as close as the poem attains to sheer comic relief. The change of tone also marks a broad shift of emphasis. The earlier tales have tended to be dominated by the characters of their tellers. Now the emphasis will be on the nature and effect of the tale itself. Rather than providing surrogates for their narrators, the protagonists of the later tales tend to be broadly comic (Sir Thopas, Chauntecleer), or radically exemplary (Melibee, Cecilie, the Monk's tragic heroes). The techniques and resources of tale-telling become a major concern, inviting us to review and reflect on the diverse strategies of earlier and more ambitious tellers.

The impulse to self-criticism is very strong in Chaucer's poetry, and nowhere more strikingly so than in the paired tales he assigns to his pilgrim narrator. *Sir Thopas*, in its vacillating movement, its contamination of the idealism of romance with bourgeois vanity and churlish violence, and the haplessness of its narrator in the face of its self-proliferating plot, is a parodic distillation of certain features of the *Canterbury Tales* as a whole. The skeletal narrative of *Melibee*, offered as a second effort after Sir Thopas has been shouted down in mid-career, is a mere frame for moral instruction, devoid of human content, its characters no more than the sum of the arguments put into their mouths. By posing the alternatives of aimless play and stultifying didacticism, the two tales define the poles between which Chaucer's various narrators locate themselves, and show him weighing the pros and cons of a radically experimental poem in which the competing claims of authority and random experience remain unresolved.

When Harry Baily suddenly turns to the pilgrim narrator, noting that his small, round figure would make an apt lady's plaything, and eliciting the timid confession that the only tale he knows is a "rhyme" learned long ago, he casts the narrator in a role oddly like that of the Prioress's little scholar, haplessly chanting his single song. Like the child, the narrator will soon be caught up in a compulsive process, powerless to control the verses he emits. Many of the innumerable ineptitudes of *Sir Thopas* seem intended to defuse with humor the tension created by the Prioress. A song "loud and cleere" like the child's anthem is here assigned to the gentle wood-dove. The "lilie flour" that is the object of the Prioress's devotion becomes part of Sir Thopas's crest, protruding from the top of a tower as if set in a vase. And a proud reference to Thopas's armor as "Jewes werk" reminds us that Jews could have a positive function in medieval society.

But the tale has broader implications. Like the framing narrative of the *Canterbury Tales*, Sir Thopas's search for the elf-queen is a quest, inspired by "love-longynge" and mirroring the larger poem's continual reversion to romance and courtly-chivalric values. The sudden discovery of the land of "faerye," hidden away in a "privy place" as if behind a bush, is like the unexpected surfacing of courtly idealism in the tales of the worldly Wife and practical Franklin. Thopas's naive quest is a lowest-common-denominator version of the plight of the courtly in the world of the poem. The tolerance it asks — more than Harry Baily, for one, is able to muster — is challenged by the sheer irresponsibility of Thopas himself, whose aimless indulgence of physical energy and sexual fantasy are in effect what remains of the chivalric enterprise in the absence of political and social values. Implicit in Thopas's adolescent sexuality is the latent violence that subverts Theseus' chivalric order. His continual "priking," interspersed as it is with sudden fits of total exhaustion, is part of the tale's peculiar charm, but it is described in terms that evoke the frenzied coupling of the Reeve's tale, and it leaves his horse's flanks streaming with blood. His elaborate arming not only indulges the narrator's guildsman-like impulse to flaunt the quality of his equipment, but reminds us that chivalric values are a façade, and threaten always to insulate the chivalric hero from the claims of ordinary humanity and the recognition of his own weakness. Thopas's naiveté is an embryonic version of the overconfidence of Theseus and the moral obtuseness of Arveragus.

The structure of *Sir Thopas*, too, is significant. Each successive "fit" is half as long as the last and contains proportionally less action (in the third, Thopas does no more than mount his horse), implying a prolongation in which action would be to structure as Achilles is to the tortoise. So in the *Tales* as a whole the theme of pilgrimage is suspended as one story-teller after another pursues his own preoccupations. When Thopas, on encountering Sir Oliphaunt, turns completely around and pricks home, his abrupt retreat mocks the retrograde movement of the larger sequence, where each descent into churlishness occasions a withdrawal to a new starting-point, and a remustering of the resources of order and authority.

In the end the narrator himself is forced to make a similar retreat. Attacked for his "rym dogerel," he responds with the prose *Melibee*, which is to *Sir Thopas* as substance to accident, a tale as relentlessly "serious" as any in the poem. The action consists almost entirely of a long, highly sententious dialogue between the young Melibeus and his wife Prudence, aimed at enabling Melibeus to forgive "adversaries" who have beaten his wife and inflicted "five mortal wounds" on his daughter, Sophie. The tale is exemplary on several levels. Identified at the outset as "myghty and riche," Melibeus is both a private individual, and endowed with legal authority and a capacity to muster forces which make him in effect a king. The tale continually shifts between the personal and the political, now balancing inner peace against private vengeance, now opposing political stability to war. The "adversaries" are glossed allegorically as the world, the flesh, and the devil, whose afflictions result from Melibeus' own sinfulness, but they are at the same time literal malefactors, whom Prudence persuades to appeal to Melibeus for forgiveness.

The mortal wounds of Melibeus' daughter Sophie, wisdom in its ideal aspect, are the *données* of the dialogue. "Left for dead" by the adversaries, she never appears, but her possible resuscitation is mentioned at several points. In her absence, Prudence, or practical wisdom, seeks to preserve Melibeus' awareness of higher reality, and we are made aware of the spiritual implications of her role. When Melibeus rejects her counsel, claiming that "wommen been wikke," her rebuttal cites the Incarnation, and the manifestation of the risen Christ to Mary Magdalene, as evidence of women's fitness to be vessels of truth. The efficacy of her "sweet words" is noted several times, and she punctuates her lessons with biblical quotations, culminating in a reminder of the apocalyptic context in which Melibeus' acts will finally be assessed, and thereby providing the cue for his final reconciliation with the adversaries.

All this may suggest a more dialectically coherent dialogue than we are actually given. The stages of a conventional *consolatio* are visible in Prudence's patient address to Melibeus' wrath, pride and hard-heartedness, but the effect is that of a list of set topics, and the non-psychological character of the story is part of Chaucer's point in telling it. Against *Sir Thopas*, in which meaning is forestalled by random incident, Chaucer has set a tale devoid of human circumstance. Melibeus has no identity: he is man in a sinful world, and hence his responses to Prudence's *sententiae* remain ambiguous: moral choice has no meaning without the fiction of a concrete human situation in which alternatives can be weighed.

These limitations are clear in the closing episodes. Persuaded by Prudence to admit their guilt and seek forgiveness, the adversaries come forward and appeal to "the excellence and benignitee of his gracious lordshipe." Melibee responds benignly, and all seems well until Prudence asks what sentence he will impose, and Melibee replies that he will strip them of their goods and exile them forever. After the long preceding dialogue this is as anticlimactic as Thopas's sudden turnaround on encountering Sir Olifaunt. But there is no basis for interpreting Melibee's sudden relapse into hostility, or the equally abrupt vanishing of the danger it poses in the final paragraphs. In a bare thirty lines Prudence induces Melibeus to use his power courteously and mercifully, ending with St. James' warning that "Juggement withouten mercy shal be doon to hym that hath no mercy of another wight" (1869). Melibeus is inwardly moved by her words: when the adversaries reappear he is merciful, and his final reflections on the Last Judgment show Prudence's words informing his deliberations. But this conclusion is less a resolution of the crisis than an alternative version. The sudden introduction of a psychological dimension points up the barrenness of what has gone before. In its net effect *Melibee* remains a set of arguments in search of a story capable of bringing them to life, and the voice we hear in Melibeus' beautiful final lines is as disembodied as that which will speak to us in the Parson's tale.

The ponderously high-minded *Melibee* is like a Knight's tale reduced to a study in abstract terms of the responsibilities embodied in Theseus. *Sir Thopas*, like the Cook's tale, breaks off after demonstrating the anarchy latent in its playfulness. The massive coherence of the one nearly suspends narrative movement, while the sheer vitality and openness of the other are all but incoherent. Nothing happens in either story, and their juxtaposition illustrates in a negative way the problem of integrating meaning with narrative form, a problem Chaucer must continually have pondered as the *Canterbury Tales* took shape. A similar balancing of alternatives appears in the paired tales of the Monk and the Nun's Priest. The Monk's book of tragedies is as ambitious as the Knight's tale in its historical sweep, but in his single-minded concern with fortune the Monk denies his tragic heroes the rich psychological and historical life that is the strength of Chaucerian characterization. The contrasting tale of the Nun's Priest is so fraught with literary allusion and moral commentary that its humble Aesopian outlines are at times hard to recognize; epic and biblical history, metaphysical speculations and the ongoing debate over marriage jostle one another to offer competing perspectives on Chauntecleer's near-disaster at the hands of the fox. The Nun's Priest, perhaps the most Chaucer-like of all the pilgrims, has created a narrator for whom the exercise of high style is an end in itself. His posturings have much in common with the brilliantly rendered vanity of Chauntecleer, and distort the moral focus of his story in a way that recalls the Monk's pompous sententiousness, calling into question the self-inflating tendency of all artistic creation on the grand scale.

The Monk's austere literary taste is hard to reconcile with the worldly and sensual "outridere" of the General Prologue. But the solemnity of his undertaking is superficial: the lives of great figures of biblical, classical and contemporary history are reduced to occasions for banal moralizing. The Monk is aware of the larger forces that shape his heroes' lives, but curiously unresponsive to them. Thus he announces Samson, the subject of his first fully rendered story, as a man consecrated to God and "annunciat" by angelic prophecy, but then focuses exclusively and repeatedly on Samson's inability to conceal secrets from his wives. The effect is to reduce the brief narrative to a tale of just desserts that ends appropriately with the hero blind and helpless at the mill. The Monk goes on to report Samson's destruction of the Philistine temple, but offers no comment on the redemptive self-sacrifice that transforms Samson's tragedy of fortune into a spiritual triumph, and ends with a final warning against confiding in one's wife. His stunted, Philistine perspective recalls the recurring humiliation that dogged the hero in his life.

The story of the death of Hercules which follows has no moral at all beyond a pointless hint that the hero's acceptance of Deianira's gift of the poisoned garment of Nessus was a failure of self-knowledge; it ends by focusing on Hercules' death throes for their own sake, with no hint of the meaning of his death for gods or mortals. And the ignoring of larger implications is even more striking in the story of Antiochus, drawn from the second book of *Maccabees*. Much space is devoted to the literal details of the wounds with which Antiochus was afflicted by God for having thought to conquer Jerusalem. Antiochus finally acknowledges God's dominion, but the single line devoted to his repentance is all but lost amid repeated references to the "stink" of his wounds, and we hear nothing of the desperate attempts to atone to God and make restitution to the Jews which are so prominent in the Monk's biblical source. A story with the character of classical tragedy is thus rendered trivial and grotesque.

A more complex example of the reductive treatment of tragic material is the story of Count Ugolino, where the Monk's alterations, set against the incomparable version of Dante's *Inferno*, his acknowledged source, stand out with particular clarity. Dante's Ugolino, imprisoned and starved to death with his sons, is a monster of egotism, and the power of his first-person narrative is enhanced by our knowledge that the teller has been damned. He is a traitor as well as a victim of treachery, and his story confirms his damnation by showing the self-absorption that made him deny his sons the compassion he now solicits for himself. Having told it, he returns to the eternal task of gnawing at the neck of his betrayer Ruggiero, and we realize that his narrative has expressed the hunger of one whose sole surviving motives are self-justification and revenge.

The Monk elaborates the pathos of the story. Hugelyn's sons become little boys; the youngest, a child of three, complains movingly of a starvation whose cause he cannot understand, and kisses his father as he dies. Ugolino, too, is altered. Where Dante's hero describes himself as "turned inwardly to stone" so that he cannot join his children in weeping, the Monk's Hugelyn weeps freely as his children die around him, suggesting a community in suffering that is wholly absent in the *Inferno*. But in fact the Monk describes a selfishness as complete as that of Dante's Ugolino. His hero shows emotion, but his feelings are only for himself. At the sound of the locking of the tower, he realizes that his enemies

"wolde doon *hym* dyen." It is for this that he weeps, and as
he gnaws at his limbs he inveighs only against Fortune's
betrayal of himself. The Monk's pathos aims to elicit sympathy for a bereaved parent, but in fact it substitutes maudlin
self-pity for the emotional void so starkly depicted in Dante's
version. The story is finally the most striking instance of the
Monk's failure to do justice to his material.

This failure is worth comparing with that of the *Melibee* in
its naive attempt to make literature out of sheer platitude. For
the pilgrim narrator, the dogmatism of Prudence or the
rambling of Sir Thopas is an end in itself, and it does not
occur to him that his literary ventures may have no bearing
on the real world. The failure of such writing is a failure of
innocence. The Monk's, by contrast, is a failure of
worldliness. His material is human history, from the primordial falls of Lucifer and Adam to events of the recent past.
He is intelligent and mature, but like his Belshazzar and
Croesus, whose wealth and power render them deaf to the
prophecies of their destruction, in gaining experience of
secular life he has lost the power to recognize it for what it
is, and so is incapable of rising above purely worldly fortune
in depicting his heroes' fates. He reduces their misfortunes to
cliché and platitude with the facility of one who disguises his
own worldliness by condemning the world.

Amid this context of failure, the tale of the Syrian queen
Zenobia, far the longest of the tragedies and the only one
devoted to a woman, is a unique success, a well-conducted
narrative whose intrinsic interest is given unusually full scope
before the anticlimactic "Allas Fortune!" with which the
Monk points his unvarying moral. The Diana-like Zenobia rejects conventional female behavior to acquire strength and
athletic skill, and when obliged to marry she restricts her sexual
relations to the minimum necessary to ensure the production
of children. Left mistress of a great empire at her husband's
death, she maintains it forcefully until seized at last by the
emperor Aurelian, forced to walk before her chariot in his
triumph, and reduced to the status of a private woman,
wielding a distaff instead of a scepter.

On the one hand Zenobia's is the story of a heroic figure whose downfall consists in being forced to accept the status of a mere woman. But it is also a story of integrity forced into contact with the world. Drawn out of her virgin life, she makes a minimal concession to conjugal duty while continuing to live by her own standards. Only when power comes into her hands at her husband's death does she break out of her self-imposed role, embarking on a new life of conquest that ends in her capture and final reduction to conventional domesticity. The Monk tells the story well, but the effect of his powerful narrative is undermined by the arbitrariness with which it is reduced in the end to yet another instance of the work of fortune. As in all Chaucer's narratives of women, a traditional authoritarianism undermines the freedom and autonomy of the heroine; but we may also sense, as in the case of Samson, Antiochus, or Hercules, an awareness on Chaucer's part that his sources harbor a more profound conception of tragedy than the Monk's authoritarianism can admit. When Chaucer allows the Monk to bungle the story of Samson he is surely inviting us to consider that story more seriously; his decision to deal with Hercules' final agony or the foul-smelling wounds of Antiochus suggest that he had read attentively the bitter questioning of divine justice by the dying Hercules of Ovid's *Metamorphoses*, and would have understood a drama like the *Philoctetes* of Sophocles.

We can see this sort of literary self-consciousness in the line that concludes the Monk's narrative of Ugolino: "From heigh estaat Fortune awey hym *carf*" (cut). The moral is utterly predictable in all but the curious verb, which reminds us that the story the Monk tells has itself been cut away, excised both from the context of known Italian history that would render Ugolino's crisis intelligible and from the intricate structure of Dante's *Commedia*. Dante, the Monk says, can tell such a story "Fro point to point" (i.e. in full detail); and for Chaucer, if not for the Monk, it was the continuity this implies, the ability to set his characters in a context of the fullest significance, spiritual and historical, that made Dante's poetry unique and revolutionary. By the standard of

Dante's seriousness, of his constant awareness of fundamental issues, the Monk's very conception of "serious" literature stands condemned, and it is worth pondering the meaning his failure may have had for Chaucer himself. The Chaucer who worries lest churls subvert the decorum of the *Canterbury Tales* also shows himself acutely aware of the dangers inherent in the more orthodox sources of his poem: not just the Monk's tale but those of the Man of Law, Clerk and Pardoner illustrate how moralization can distort or obfuscate social and political reality in the process of interpreting it. Chaucer is always in total control of these conventional materials, and brilliant in turning them against themselves; but in his exposure of the Monk there may lurk the embarrassment of a poet keenly aware of the achievement of Dante, and correspondingly aware of the limitations of his own older-fashioned poetic tradition. In judging the Monk by the standard of the *Commedia* Chaucer is perhaps exercising a prescience of which he was fully capable, and judging medieval poetry for a moment by the standard of the Renaissance.

The Nun's Priest's tale, coming at the end of a series of tales that expose the weaknesses of medieval literary modes, shows poetry at its most "medieval" making a strong comeback. Its basis is the Aesopian fable of the cock and the fox, a narrative that can easily be told in two or three hundred words. What swells Chaucer's version to some 600 lines is the narrator's insistence on giving it the trappings of "serious" poetry, a combination of style and superadded subject matter which defers the main story for 400 lines and defies us to locate its real substance. Ostensibly this added content tells us how Chauntecleer should have prepared himself to meet the fox, and how we should understand his failure to do so, but it does other things as well. On the one hand it shows how art can inflate both the importance of what it describes and the self-importance of the artist. The power of rhetoric, the illusion it creates of controlling the world, is as symptomatic of pride as Chauntecleer's sense of being lord of the barnyard and herald of the sun. But at the same time the Nun's Priest's beneficent charm and the homely world he describes may seduce us into simply enjoying the action and its setting for their own sake. So all-encompassing is this extraordinary tale that it evokes the vast philosophical perspectives and deep anxieties of the Knight and Man of Law by means of a fable that has the miniaturized charm and clockwork perfection of the Miller's Oxenford.

From the opening lines we see style straining to outgrow the limits of the humble story. Ostensibly they set up the simple life of the poor widow as a foil to the mock-sumptuousness of Chauntecleer's, but the narrator manages to develop this unpromising theme at some length, almost, it seems, in spite of himself:

Three large sowes hadde she, and namo,[1]	[1] no more
Three keen,[1] and eek a sheep that highte Malle.	[1] cows
Full sooty was hire bour and eek hir halle,	
In which she eet ful many a sklendre[1] meel.	[1] meagre
Of poynaunt[1] sauce hir needed never a deel.[2]	[1] spicy [2] bit
No deyntee morsel passed thurgh hir throte;	
Hir diete was accordant to hir cote.[1]	[1] cottage
Repleccioun[1] ne made hire nevere sik;	[1] overeating
Attempree[1] diete was al hir phisik,	[1] moderate
And exercise, and hertes suffisaunce.	
The goute lette hire nothyng for to daunce,	
N'apoplexie shente[1] nat hir heed.	[1] hurt, harmed
No wyn ne drank she, neither whit ne reed;	
Hir bord was served moost with whit and blak, −	
Milk and broun breed, in which she foond no lak,	
Seynd[1] bacoun, and somtyme an ey[2] or tweye;[3]	[1] smoked [2] egg [3] two
For she was, as it were, a maner deye.[1]	[1] dairywoman

(VII.2830–46)

The detailed inventory of the widow's humble resources makes it hard to focus on their humbleness, and the naming of her sheep, charming in itself, is a further distraction. As the narrator dwells on what the widow does *not* eat and drink, and the ills she therefore does not incur, his tone grows self-important, and his rhetoric begins to assume its own momentum. The report of her actual diet returns us to straightforward moralizing, but the introduction of bacon and the occasional egg is a new complication, and the final line, hinting that the widow is not, after all, wholly cut off from the world of commerce, has the gratuitously confiding tone of village gossip. At one moment we are drawn away from the moral essence of the widow's life by a pointlessly grandiose rhetoric (the "diet" passage, for all its prosaic subject matter, has the tone of the Man of Law or the Monk). At another, like tourists in the hands of a skillful guide, we are experiencing this simple world with an intimacy and knowingness that disarm moral awareness. Both tendencies are mirrored in Chauntecleer. His many-colored splendor, set against the black-and-white of the widow's world, assumes colossal stature when his crowing is compared to a church organ, its regularity to that of a tower clock, and his comb to a crenellated rampart. The poet endows the bird with learning, chivalry and a kind of spirituality, but interposes these with the precisely rendered strutting, chuck-chucking, and sudden flurryings of a real rooster. The grandiosity and the humility are equally seductive, and we are no more bothered than the cock himself by the glaring contrast between style and substance.

Chauntecleer also has his sober side. His dream of the fox begins the action of the tale, and we are taken aback when this splendid absurdity suddenly groans, with the unnerving authenticity of "man that in his dreem is drecched [troubled] soore," and prays to God for protection. The accents are those of the *anima naturaliter christiana*, and his half-formed sense that the creature of his dream sought to murder him makes us forget that a rooster is talking. He goes on to rebut the strident skepticism of his wife, the hen Pertelote, on the subject of dreams (she suggests that what he needs is a laxative) with a spare, powerful story that shows him unexpectedly capable of seriousness.

Two wealthy pilgrims are forced to take separate lodgings for the night, and one is visited with a series of dreams that report the murder of the other. Twice the dreamer fails to respond when his fellow appears, announcing his imminent death and appealing for aid. But when in a third dream the

pilgrim, now dead, describes his murder and explains how it
may be exposed, he finally acts; in the end the corpse is
recovered and the murderers are caught and hanged.

Powerful in itself, the story is also Chaucer's one example
of a fully successful exercise in the rhetoric of affective piety.
The dreamer's initial unresponsiveness is set off by the
vividness of the appeal to his fellow-feeling ("Now help me,
deere brother, or I dye"), and what finally moves him is
largely the Christ-like apparition of the murdered man
("Bihoold my bloody woundes, depe and wyde!"), with his
"ful pitous face, pale of hewe." As he cries out for justice,
the dreamer imagines his friend's corpse, "gaping upryght"
amid the cartload of dung in which it is concealed, suggesting
how efficiently the dream has stimulated his sense of the horror of the act. Other details that might have been gratuitous
in a less disciplined tale here reinforce the central purpose.
The dung-cart is not just a nasty place to conceal the body,
like the Jewish privy in the Prioress's tale; its purpose is in its
very ordinariness, the deceptive innocence with which it
trundles toward the city gate on its way "as it were to donge
lond." And when the tale ends with a jerk, as the murderers
are "hanged by the neck-bone," the effect is to reinforce the
justice which is the final effect of the dreamer's attentiveness
to his dream. In a tale largely concerned with the aberrant
tendencies of literary language, this brief story offers a standard of functionality for moral fiction.

But Chauntecleer is as vulnerable as his narrator to the
seductions of eloquence. As he goes on to relate other stories,
the force with which he insists on the folly of neglecting
dreams becomes an end in itself. Of the child-king Kenelm of
Murcia, whose death was foretold to him in a symbolic
dream, Chauntecleer declares that his youth made him
heedless of the prophecy, though in the legend he osten-
tatiously professes to have read Kenelm not only accepts his
prophesied death but collaborates with the agents of his passion in Christ-like resignation. By the end of the ensuing
parade of biblical and classical examples, even the cock's
own impending misfortune has become the occasion for a

rhetorical flourish, a crescendo which builds to a final dismissal of Pertelote, her advice, and her laxatives. The net effect of the long speech is to renew Chauntecleer's *amour propre*. Then, like the inflated object that he is, he descends gradually into the barnyard world again, to pursue the necessities of sex and food. He has become himself an exemplary figure, "royal as a prince" in his own view, and as blind in his pomp as the Monk's Belshazzar.

Even now, well over half-way through the tale, we are only on the threshold of the story proper, which begins as elaborately as the General Prologue, comparing the idyllic bliss of Chauntecleer and Pertelote to the Edenic beginnings of earthly life. But amid the aggrandizing rhetoric, Chauntecleer's sudden "Cok! cok!" at the sight of the fox recalls us to the fallen world, and the comparison to "man that was affrayed in his herte" suggests again the incipiently spiritual sense of evil that had informed his response to his dream. The fox has all the astuteness and false good will of the fiend in the Friar's tale, and fully justifies the narrator's warning to princes on the perils of flattery.

But as Chauntecleer, dazzled by the fox's praising of his wisdom and grandeur, is being lured toward his exemplary downfall, the narrator is attempting to rise to the occasion by treating the story as a tragedy with profound implications. At the first appearance of the fox he withdraws from the action for a time to raise large questions about the significance of dreams, the relation of human free will to God's foreordaining of events, and the relations of men and women. These are questions which Chaucer takes seriously in other contexts, and they may seem to provide us with the sort of sustained reflection on the causes and implications of tragedy that had been so conspicuously lacking in the Monk's tale. But in fact the passage offers not a coherent perspective on the story but a series of possible perspectives, each of which ends by more or less cancelling out the one preceding. The fox is a Judas, a Ganelon, a Sinon. Chauntecleer was warned by his dream that this was a fatal day. But the event was foreknown by God, and perhaps predestined, in which case both the

malignity of the fox and the augury of the dream are meaningless. But the tale must have a moral: Chauntecleer (let us
say, though the story does not show us precisely this) allowed
his wife to advise him, as Adam did, and this is often
hazardous. But do not suppose that I am speaking seriously
in suggesting that a woman could cause harm:

> Thise been the cokkes wordes, and nat myne;
> I kan noon harm of no womman divyne.
> (VII.3265–66)

Passing swiftly through the roles of moral tragedian,
philosopher and preacher, the narrator discovers himself at
last in the role of "courteous" poet, more worried about his
obligation to the social graces than about the meaning of his
story. Each new pose draws us further away from the moral
essence of Chauntecleer's situation, and the final attempt to
fob off on the cock himself the consequences of the narrator's
moralism shows him helpless in the face of his own platitudes,
like the narrator of *Sir Thopas* beset by the clichés of popular
romance.

As the story proceeds, the narrator's guileless preten-
tiousness hovers over the action like a balloon, no more clearly
focused on Chauntecleer's situation than the tale of little King
Kenelm. When Chauntecleer is finally seized by the fox, the
Nun's Priest pulls out all the stops:

> O destinee, that mayst nat been eschewed!
> Allas, that Chauntecleer fleigh fro the bemes![1]   [1] rafters
> Allas, his wyf ne roght[1] nat of dremes!   [1] cared
> And on a Friday fil al this meschaunce.
> (VII.3338–41)

Summing up his earlier meditation on the possible causes of
the cock's tragedy in a bare three lines, without in any way
resolving the questions involved, the narrator pursues his
rhetoric into new realms of irrelevance. Friday is Venus' day,
yet Venus had no care for her servant Chauntecleer. On
Friday King Richard the Lionhearted was slain (it was also
traditionally the day of the Flood, the Crucifixion, and other

biblical disasters) and Geoffrey of Vinsauf, in his treatise on
the art of poetry, attacked the day itself in the course of a
long lament for Richard designed to show other poets how to
"pleyne." Turning from the central event to invoke first the
day, then the goddess of the day, and finally a school-poet
who had railed against the day, is a strong comment on the
limited power of poetry, which can "do" nothing about the
tragic events it presumes to engage, and is apt to delude itself
even about its ability to interpret them.

But there is a sense in which the Nun's Priest's inflated
rhetoric, by magnifying the implications of his story, serves
also to clarify them. At the heart of both Geoffrey's lament
for Richard and the narrator's anxiety about dreams and
destiny is an instinct as fundamental as that which moves
Chauntecleer to piety in the aftermath of his dream, the in-
stinctive need for order. At this lowest-common-denominator
level, prayer, philosophical speculation and moral sententiousness are all no more than rhetoric, ways of evading the
horror of total uncertainty.

In this regard a crucial moment in the story is that which
describes the exposure of the murder in Chauntecleer's own
first exemplary tale. It is the heart of the Nun's Priest's tale
psychologically, a serious response to a powerful visionary
experience. But the response is typical of the rhetoric of this
tale, in that it takes the form of an outcry:

> "I crye out on the ministres," quod he,
> That sholden kepe and reulen this citee.
> Harrow! allas! heere lith my felawe slayn!"
> (VII.3043–45)

The appeal is instantly effective. Concerted popular action
discovers the corpse, and official justice quickly follows,
enabling Chauntecleer to declare that "mordre wol out." But
just as the dream in Chauntecleer's narrative is a uniquely efficient medium of vision, explicit and compelling in its effect,
so the outcry it evokes, translating nightmare directly into
coherent political discourse, is uniquely and implausibly
efficacious as a form of action. In themselves the pilgrim's
words are hardly more a political act than Chauntecleer's own

"Cok! cok!" The strange blend of fear, prayer, and sententious advice to princes is essentially the expression of a
psychological need, an attempt to attain private stability by
the invocation of public order. The pilgrim's gesture provides
a key to the relationship between the frame of tragic rhetoric
the Nun's Priest constructs for his story and the situation of
Chauntecleer within it. For all its grandiosity, the rhetoric of
the tale does perform a function for the anxious mind by invoking the paradigms of order, even if only in a tentative or
negative way. One way in which it does this is by elevating the
humble story to the dignity of tragedy, which, if it cannot explain the secret causes of our misfortunes, can at least, when
effectively deployed, compel us to reflect on them. The
Nun's Priest's tact is flawless: it is never precisely his story or
its hero that we take seriously. But he manages to convey the
reality of our own moral experience and remind us of real
dangers inherent in the state of half-awareness most of us
inhabit most of the time. A poem that mocks the world-
historical and Dantean pretensions of the Monk becomes in
its own way an apology for "serious" poetry.

But the limited efficacy of the order created by rhetoric is
also made plain. The result of the actual theft of the cock is
a breakdown of order in which the widow's austere life is
utterly disrupted, domestic animals run wild, and language itself
is reduced to mere noise:

Certes he Jakke Straw and his meynee[1]	[1] followers
Ne made nevere shoutes half so shrille	
Whan that they wolden any Flemyng kille,	
As thilke[1] day was maad upon the fox.	[1] that
Of bras they broghten bemes,[1] and of box,[2]	[1] trumpets
	[2] boxwood
Of horn, of boon,[1] in which they blewe and	[1] bone
powped,[2]	[2] puffed
And therewithal they skriked[1] and they	[1] shrieked
howped.[2]	[2] whooped
It semed as that hevene sholde falle.	

(VII.3394–401)

The chaos and cacophony are to the narrator's earlier rhetorical sallies as the Knight's account of Arcite's funeral is

to his celebration of the chivalry of Theseus, and like the funeral they suggest a primal horror lurking beneath the flurry of panic-stricken activity.

Like the recalling of Geoffrey's lament for Richard, the name of "Jack Straw," synonymous with the violence of the peasant uprisings of 1381, intrudes a note of unnerving authenticity. By punctuating his opposition between seemingly irrelevant rhetoric and particularized realism with the two most explicit references to English history in all of Chaucer, the Nun's Priest challenges us to recognize the larger reality these events comprise. Richard Lionheart was the stuff of legend, his life enveloped in an aura of idealized chivalry and crusading piety, as distant from the concrete realities of contemporary life as the Knight's treatment of Theseus. But he was also an English ruler whose adventures, like the royal campaigns of Chaucer's own day, involved exploiting his subjects and neglecting the business of kingship. The Nun's Priest is serious about history, and his balancing of the distant memory of regicide with the revolts of 1381, the most shocking political event of his own time, recalls the speech of the Knight's Saturn, for whom conflict is the governing principle of life and history, and "the churls' rebelling" is an equal and opposite reaction to order imposed arbitrarily from above. Heaven does not fall in the Nun's Priest's tale, and many booby-traps lie waiting for anyone who would take it too seriously, but when the story ends with Chauntecleer's sudden adroit escape from the clutches of the fox, we are left with a disconcerting sense of both the crucial importance and the limited scope of individual initiative in the face of an uncertain reality. The Nun's Priest's genial invitation to locate the substance of his narrative, to "take the fruit and let the chaff be still," can seem almost a taunt.

Chapter 7

The final tales

In the final tales the probing of the limitations of Chaucer's own art that characterizes the tales considered in the previous chapters is developed in moral and spiritual terms. There is a precise thematic opposition between the Canon's Yeoman's tale of the desperate, failed, and finally specious project of alchemical "translation" undertaken by his mad scientists, who seek to make gold from dross, and the lucid depiction of spiritual transformation in the immediately preceding tale of the Second Nun. The implicit contrast between Cecilie's fulfillment through faith and the failure of the Canon's earthly magic is reinforced by the bitterness with which the Yeoman recalls his own close involvement in the Canon's obsession; he has given his life to a finally abortive quest, and his disillusionment suggests a deeper skepticism as to the value of such syntheses as human art can attain. The Manciple's tale, which follows, is the most extreme of Chaucer's many attempts to incorporate a philistine perspective into the larger poem. It is prefaced by a scene in which the Manciple mocks the drunken Cook, and his easy victory over one who has forfeited the dignity of speech and self-governance prepares us for a tale that seems to confirm Chaucer's early misgivings about his undertaking in the *Tales*: churldom triumphs over courtliness, worth and beauty are destroyed by wrath, and love is reduced to infidelity and violent jealousy.

The concluding reflections of the Yeoman's Plato suggest in a peculiarly moving way the ultimate futility of the ingenuity embodied in human art, and the Manciple's malicious reflections on the helplessness of his wrathful Phoebus Apollo seem calculated to exorcise through mockery any idealism we may still harbor regarding the value of human speech. Together the two tales create an increasingly somber mood that prepares us for the treatise of the Parson, in which all human endeavor not directed toward living virtuously in the sight of God is dismissed as meaningless.

The Canon's Yeoman's tale is unique in the extent to which it reflects the teller's own experience. He and his master do not make their sudden appearance until the Second Nun has concluded her tale, and hence he knows nothing of the game the pilgrims are playing. What he offers is less a "tale" than a response to the Host's request for information about the Canon and his alchemical work. His account of his service with the Canon overflows his prologue and fills the "prima pars" of the tale, and he is well into the "pars secunda" or tale proper when it suddenly occurs to him to explain that the wholly dishonest canon-alchemist he is now describing is not his own master. The attempt at authorial distancing seems oddly gratuitous. Morally speaking, the distinction between the two canons is at best a matter of degree: the Yeoman has declared that all alchemists are more or less dishonest, and his master has fled in fear that the Yeoman will reveal the truth about his work. It is likely that there is as much of the Yeoman's master in the wholly false canon of "pars secunda" as in the desperately hopeful experimenter of the prologue and "prima pars," and it is probable, too, that the Yeoman cannot separate them in his own mind.

Certainly the Yeoman's attitude toward his master is ambivalent. His persistent use of "we" in describing the endless search for the true "craft" shows him closely identified with the Canon's quest, but he has been left hopelessly in debt and permanently disfigured, and clearly feels betrayed by his master has fled in fear that the Yeoman will reveal the truth creation of an unambiguously wicked pseudo-alchemist may be a way of exorcising any lingering feelings of sympathy, and isolating the aspect of the Canon by which he feels himself to have been wronged. But at the end of "pars secunda" he undoes his distinction between the two canons again, and combines what little wisdom he has gleaned from his own experience with the obvious moral of his story of the false canon, suggesting that the larger force at work in both cases is the incorrigible desire for gold. He cannot clearly distinguish alchemy from fraud, or separate his own pursuit of its secrets from the greed of the stylish priest who is duped by the false canon. Each failure of "translation" gives rise to a renewal of the attempt and to further moral confusion. At each new stage there is more unfulfilled desire to be rationalized, and the peculiar self-perpetuating power of the chain of alchemy's false promises expresses the delusive appeal of earthly life.

The final ninety lines of the tale, a meditation on alchemy as eloquent as any philosophical passage in Chaucer, make it clear that he is not wholly dismissive of the search for the quintessential synthesis. The aspiration to refine away the dross of materiality by scientific means has a certain dignity, like the Knight's attempt to create a world order out of chivalry, or the Wife's fantasy of attaining sexual harmony in gentilesse. But whereas these projects show human nature seeking to rise above itself and create transcendent value, alchemy is utterly secular in its aspirations, willfully confined to the material world and almost inevitably contaminated by greed. Like money itself, it corrupts the relations of human beings with nature, God, and one another. The Yeoman, in whom the "fresh and red" of youth has become the color of lead, embodies the degrading effects of materialism, reduced to the condition of the very elements he seeks to transform.

The solemn exaltation of the concluding discourse of Plato and his disciple bring the full implications of the Yeoman's narrative into view. Plato himself, momentarily endowed with the spirit of prophecy, is made to declare that access to the secrets of nature is wholly in the power of Christ. There is something implausible about the Yeoman's sudden ascent to a timeless, philosopher's perspective on his story in the final stages; it parallels the odd privileging of the vision of Plato, and the two together suggest strongly that Chaucer is speaking through his fictional narrator, laying aside his wand to comment on the finally specious character of all mere art, and any claim to knowledge not informed by the light of a higher truth. To attain such truth on the basis of earthly science alone would be to possess a secret like that *Magnasia*, a perfect synthesis of the four elements, whose constitution, Plato says, philosophers were long ago forbidden to impart to the world:

> For unto Crist it is so lief[1] and deere   [1] beloved
> That he ne wol that it discovered bee,
> But where it liketh to his deitee
> Men for t'enspire, and eek for to deffende[1]   [1] prohibit
> Whom that hym liketh; lo, this is the ende.
> (VIII.1467–71)

Here the Canon's Yeoman is of course saying far more than he knows, and the somber wisdom that informs his words expresses Chaucer's final, circumscribing judgment on the capacities of human art.

The moral weight and human appeal of the Yeoman's confession are in stark contrast to the mean-spiritedness of the Manciple, and the flawed idealism of the alchemists becomes almost noble when juxtaposed with the Manciple's tale of a world where aspiration has no place. It is the story of Phoebus, his wife, and a crow who exposes the wife's infidelity with "a man of little reputation," leading Phoebus, first, to slay his wife in sudden anger, then to seek a futile vengeance by punishing the crow. Phoebus is the embodiment of *gentilesse*, wisdom and eloquence, and the infiltration of his world by the Manciple and his values is the literary equivalent of the Manciple's own embezzlements as described in the General Prologue.

The gist of the Manciple's tale is that it is better to keep silent than to speak, and allowing him so nearly the last word is Chaucer's almost brutal means of conveying, one last time, the painful lesson that in the end even the greatest art is futile. Like the Yeoman, the Manciple cites Plato, but he does so only to justify his accurate naming of the sordid details of his story: a world in which human nature, as represented by Phoebus' wife, prefers a man of low degree to the god of light and beauty is an anti-Platonic world. The Manciple's stance recalls the narrator of the General Prologue, forced to abandon idealism and place his language at the service of a society of churls. The Manciple's world is naturalistic from the outset, but even its naturalism is debased: he compares the infidelity of Phoebus' wife successively with the impulse of a caged bird to escape to the wild and eat worms; the desire of a pampered cat to devour mice rather than milk and choice meats; the lust of a she-wolf to mate with the "lewdest" and most ignominious of males. Insidiously he implies that moral and social distinctions have no meaning: it is the nature of mankind to be attracted to "lower thing." As we are several times reminded, the wife betrays not only Phoebus, but his worth, beauty and *gentilesse*. When he retaliates in anger his music is destroyed, and his speech reduced to the empty rhetoric that denies his wife's guilt and bemoans his own folly. Any redeeming perspective on women or marriage has been foreclosed, and the narrative ends with the wholly negative gesture by which the tell-tale crow is robbed of his white feathers and sweet voice.

It is tempting to see in the fate of Phoebus' crow, the loss of both its pristine beauty and its capacity to "countrefete the speche of any man," an image of Chaucer's doubt about his own artistic project, a hint at the folly of any attempt to serve a higher end through the faithful representation of social reality. If poetry can serve truth, it would seem, the truth it conveys is all too apt to be unwelcome and degrading, and poetry subverts its own authority to the extent that it exposes the vulnerability of the fundamental decencies of courtesy and good faith: to devalue these is to authorize the Manciple's view of life. Hence the aggressive mockery with which the Manciple, in his final fifty lines, harps on the example of the crow and the wisdom of holding one's tongue. The advice has been withheld until it is too late, and the poet has already been forced into a kind of collaboration in Phoebus' betrayal.

The Manciple does acknowledge that speech is required if we are to pray and do honor to God. Coming from the Manciple such advice is bound to sound smug, but it is the only hint of redemption he offers, and so serves to effect the transition from the world of the poem thus far to that of the Parson's tale. The Parson's prose treatise on penitence and

the deadly sins, devoid of fiction or narrative, confronts us
with a final structural opposition, this time between the tem-
poral, fluid, often radically subjective vision of narrative fiction and the unchanging truths of religious doctrine. The
transition is carefully prepared: the shadows are lengthening
as the Manciple concludes, and the Host's appeal to the
Parson makes plain that his tale will conclude the tale-telling.
The Parson's promise of a "merry tale" that will "knitte up
al this feeste, and make an ende" also implies an integrative
function, but he prefaces it by forcefully rejecting "fables
and such wretchedness," and reintroducing, for the first time
since the General Prologue, the idea of pilgrimage:

> To shewe[1] you the wey, in this viage,[2]   [1] show [2] journey
> Of thilke[1] parfit[2] glorious pilgrymage   [1] that [2] perfect
> That highte[1] Jerusalem celestial.   [1] is called
>   (X.49–51)

Authority could not be reasserted in stronger terms: it is an
authority that bears equally on all, and the obligation and
promise it defines are unifying as nothing else could be.

But despite the radical shift of emphasis that it introduces,
the Parson's tale is not wholly dissociated from the body of
the poem. Its ultimate concern is with the communion of the
saints in heaven, but it has much to say about earthly community as well — friendship, the necessity and limits of social
hierarchy, and the need for "suffraunce" in human relations.
We are reminded that lordship, service, thralldom and
rebellion are metaphors for spiritual relationships, but they
are also addressed in concrete social terms, and the Parson
shows himself acutely aware of the abuses to which rank and
power were liable, and the effects these abuses could have on
the disenfranchised. Virtually every excess noted in the
behavior of the pilgrims of the General Prologue finds its cor-
rective in the Parson's inventory of vicious conduct.

But the very scope of the penitential manual, by definition
a *summa* of moral conduct, renders arbitrary any attempt to
make the Parson's tale a key to the meaning of the poem. It
is equally arbitrary to argue, as some have, that we should
view the Parson with the same ironic detachment as other

pilgrims, and that he is thereby revealed as dogmatic and tedious. It is difficult to know how to deal with a figure whose defining trait is the perfection with which he fulfills the responsibilities of his office. Much of the significance of the *Canterbury Tales* is in the complexity of the social and psychological context in which its characters move and view their lives, and certainly the absence of such a context in the Parson's observations on sin and duty is limiting as well as clarifying: after Chaucer's powerful dramatization of the problematic status of women, in society and within marriage, it is hard to simply acquiesce in the Parson's spare and categorical injunctions on the marriage-debt.

How far to go in attempting to revalue the previous tales in the light of the Parson's rejection of them is a question all readers must decide for themselves. But even if we stop short of taking it as a definitive comment on the world of the *Tales*, the Parson's discourse by its very nature invites us to reflect on the limits of that world, and it is perhaps best to view his tale as ending the poem, on Chaucer's behalf as well as his own, with a reminder of the end of human life. The world of the earlier tales is precisely "the world," where our life is lived but from which we must finally turn away.

The "Retraction" which follows the Parson's tale reinforces this sense of finality. Here Chaucer, apparently speaking in his own voice, reviews his career, acknowledges a sense of shame at having written, among other worldly writings, those of the *Canterbury Tales* "that tend to sinfulness," as well as "many a song and many a lecherous lay," and expresses his wish to make a good end. That the Retraction is to be taken at face value has been questioned on various grounds. Such gestures are not uncommon as conclusions to medieval literary works; the phrase that refers to songs and lays sounds itself suspiciously like a line of lyric verse; and there is an odd vagueness in Chaucer's reference to the works he thinks will do him credit, "books of legends of saints, and homilies, and morality, and devotion," by contrast with the careful naming of the works of "worldly vanity" that he condemns. Like Augustine's condemnation of his youthful reading of Vergil in the *Confessions*, the narrator's attempt to dismiss his secular writings seems to render them all the more vividly present, both to his mind and to us. In all likelihood the Retraction was written at the very end of Chaucer's life, and it expresses even more clearly than the Parson's tale the impulse of a mind intent on the last things, but even these final words are part of his uncompleted project.

Chapter 8

Afterword: The reception of the *Canterbury Tales*

Chaucer was the major poet of his time, and it is clear from the number of surviving manuscripts and Caxton's two early printings that the *Canterbury Tales* were his most popular work, but they were not widely imitated, and in a time when the proprietary claims of authorship were treated very casually, remarkably few attempts were made to augment them, beyond the construction by scribal editors of links among existing tales. In some manuscripts the Cook's abortive tale is supplemented by *Gamelyn*, a popular romance in loose accentual verse about a young man of noble birth forced by adversity to become a sort of Robin Hood. A single manuscript includes the broadly similar but inferior tale of *Beryn*, adapted to the structure of the *Tales* by way of a long prologue which narrates the doings of the various pilgrims after their arrival in Canterbury. The narrator is careful to make the behavior of the different pilgrims conform superficially to their Chaucerian characters, and develops a sort of fabliau around the Pardoner, who is led by an ill-considered display of sexual bravado into a nocturnal adventure that ends in his being beaten by the lover of a barmaid at his inn. John Lydgate's *Siege of Thebes*, though clearly intended as an independent work, has a similar preface which begins with a humorous imitation of the opening of the General Prologue (the main verb shows up in line 66), and describes Lydgate's encounter with the pilgrims at Canterbury.

That the relatively crude *Gamelyn* and *Beryn* were incorporated into the *Tales* suggests that the poem was seen as being of a lower order than Chaucer's other works. Such distinctions were important in the fifteenth century, when literacy was expanding to include a middle class respectful of high culture and eager to assimilate the tastes of the upper classes. England was politically isolated, French was in decline, and the vast projects of fifteenth-century writers like Lydgate and Malory reflect the desire for English versions of the major texts of continental courtly culture. In such circumstances Chaucer's realism and comic irony were bound to be undervalued, and he was regarded chiefly as a moralist, court poet, and translator. The tales that appear most often in manuscript anthologies are those of the Clerk and Prioress, and we may assume that they were read as straightforward examples of religious eloquence. Poets endlessly imitated Chaucer's earlier poems, drew courtly motifs from the tales of Knight and Squire, and echoed Chaucer's moral rhetoric, but, apart from certain of Henryson's *fables*, none directly engaged the *Tales* in their fullness and variety.

An anonymous *Plowman's Tale*, a satire on the Church establishment whose title probably owes more to Langland's Piers than to Chaucer's pilgrim, was incorporated into the *Tales* in William Thynne's edition of 1542, highlighting for post-Reformation readers the traces of anti-clericalism in the poem. Other such works were attributed to Chaucer, and he enjoyed a brief vogue as a political radical. But the "scurrility" of the *Tales* was also noted, and "Canterbury Tale" came to denote any trivial, outrageous, or bawdy story. Throughout the sixteenth century, moreover, Chaucer's language and meter were growing steadily more obscure; the situation was not improved by the attempts of Renaissance editors to correct them, and it was inevitably the more colloquial, less conventional tales that suffered most, and were least read as a result.

The traditional view of an essentially courtly Chaucer was inherited and perpetuated by Wyatt and Sidney. Even Spenser, who read Chaucer with care, and assimilated his style and language to an extraordinary degree, is remarkably sparing in his use of the non-courtly tales. The *Shepheardes Calender* at several points evokes Chaucer in his largely misattributed role as proto-Reformer, and the social criticism of *Mother Hubberds Tale* is broadly reminiscent of several of Chaucer's non-courtly tales, but Book Four of the *Faerie*

Queene, explicitly conceived as the completion of the Squire's tale, represents both Spenser's most elaborate use of Chaucer and the fullest flowering of the tradition of the courtly Chaucer.

A similarly one-sided view of Chaucer appears in the early drama. The Elizabethan period saw plays based broadly on the Clerk's, Physician's, Knight's, Man of Law's, and Franklin's tales, and even one *De Meliboeo Chauceriano*, but only Shakespeare seems to have drawn on the comic tales. In addition to the clear debt of *A Midsummer Night's Dream* and *The Two Noble Kinsmen* to the Knight's tale, it is very likely that the quarrel of Oberon and Titania in the *Dream* owes something to the figures of Pluto and Proserpina in the Merchant's tale, and that the Wife of Bath's prologue was an important model for the Falstaff of *The Merry Wives of Windsor*. Allusions to most of the *Tales* have been discovered in the plays, and it seems clear that Shakespeare was better read in Chaucer than any writer of his time save Spenser.

The courtly Chaucer is still a canonical figure for Milton's *Penseroso*, but his importance seems to have dwindled over the course of the seventeenth century. Perhaps the first post-Elizabethan writer to take Chaucer seriously, and certainly one of the first to regard the *Canterbury Tales* as his major achievement, was John Dryden, whose *Fables* (1700) include modern versions of the Knight's, Nun's Priest's, and Wife of Bath's tales. His famous Preface credits Chaucer with a representation of the world of his time, and of human nature in general, so complete and so accurate that " 'Tis sufficient to say, according to the proverb, that *here is God's Plenty*." For Dryden Chaucer's verse is irredeemably rough, a product of the "infancy of our [English] poetry," and his tone unnecessarily coarse, but he did not hesitate to declare Chaucer superior to Ovid, both in his representation of character and in the disciplined simplicity of a style in which fidelity to nature always takes precedence over "the turn of words." In Dryden's renderings his own Augustan style tends to contaminate this simplicity with unnecessary epithets, but his appreciation of the *Tales* did much to define later views of

Chaucer. After Dryden it was the poet's realism that was valued above all, a complete reversal of the Renaissance view of the poet. An early nineteenth-century biographer dismissed *Troilus and Criseyde* as "merely a love-tale," and though the *Troilus* has survived this slight, the modern editor F. N. Robinson could still place the courtly Chaucer in perspective by declaring that the love-allegory of his early poetry was "essentially foreign to his genius," a fashion which he outgrew as his work matured. In effect Chaucer came to be seen as having evolved, rather abruptly, from a medieval poet to a harbinger of the modern novel. Only in the last thirty years, and with the help of Charles Muscatine's *Chaucer and the French Tradition*, have we come to recognize the essential continuity of Chaucer's work, and the importance for the *Canterbury Tales* of the continual interplay between courtly romance and fabliau, high and low styles.

Chaucer's popularity in our own day is largely due to the scholarly enterprise of the past century, which has given us a reliable version of Chaucer's text and language, but this subject cannot be dealt with briefly. Suffice it to say that the work of the Chaucer Society, founded by F. J. Furnivall in 1867, led to the landmark editions of W. W. Skeat (1894) and F. N. Robinson (1933, 1957), and we now take for granted a range of well-annotated texts which enable us to read Chaucer in "the original," and give us a fair approximation of the sound and rhythm of his verse.

Under these fortunate circumstances we need not accept Dryden's view of Chaucer as a "rough diamond" who requires the polish of modern verse in order to be appreciated, and it can be asked whether English-speaking readers have any use for translations. These inevitably tend less to facilitate access to the original than to replace it, offering canned peaches when fresh ones are ready to hand. Setting a passage you have enjoyed, however imperfectly, in Middle English side by side with a modern rendering of it is bound to heighten the effect of the one by showing how much the other has failed to deliver.

An interesting test case is Wordsworth's rendering of the

Prioress's tale, in one sense surely the most faithful translation of Chaucer ever made. Wordsworth's feeling for the
special qualities of the tale was good (though one might wish
to rephrase his prefatory remark that "the fierce bigotry of
the Prioress forms a fine background for her tender-hearted
sympathies with the Mother and Child"), and he took great
pains to make his version as nearly as possible a transparent
medium. With the help of accent-marks Wordsworth created
a remarkable approximation of Chaucer's meter, and he
deliberately preserves archaic words (what he calls "sprinkl-
ings of antiquity") when their sense is still clear. The result
is a version that sounds superficially very much like Chaucer.
But as Theodore Morrison remarks (in an excellent introduction to his own volume of translations), it is somehow stuffy.
What comes across most clearly is the scholarly effort involved in the recreation, and its final effect is to make
Chaucer himself sound pedantic.

Morrison's own freer verse renderings, and those of Nevill
Coghill, reflect the translators' appreciation of Chaucer in a
more spontaneous way. Both are artistic achievements in their
own right, and a reader who knows the *Canterbury Tales* well
can gain real pleasure from seeing what they have done. But
the most useful service my own little book could perform
would be to help persuade those reading the *Tales* for the first
time that the use of any translation whatever is more likely to
hinder than to enhance their appreciation of Chaucer.

Guide to further reading

The standard edition of Chaucer's works is *The Riverside Chaucer*, ed. Larry D. Benson (Cambridge MA, 1987), based on that of F. N. Robinson (2nd ed., Cambridge MA, 1957); the text is accompanied by glosses and augmented by full endnotes. Good student editions are *Chaucer's Major Poetry*, ed. A. C. Baugh (New York, 1963), with an excellent introduction to Chaucer's language; and *Chaucer's Poetry: An Anthology for the Modern Reader*, ed. E. T. Donaldson (2nd ed., New York, 1975), where the poems are accompanied by critical discussion. A good cheap edition of the *Canterbury Tales* is that of A. C. Cawley (New York, 1975).

General literary background is provided by J. A. Burrow, *Medieval Writers and their Work: Middle English Literature and Its Background* (Oxford, 1982). Janet Coleman, *Medieval Readers and Writers, 1350–1400* (London, 1981), is informative on vernacular literacy, lay education, and the "literature of social unrest." The religious context of Chaucer's poetry is explored in D. W. Robertson, Jr., *A Preface to Chaucer* (Princeton NJ, 1962), which tends to reduce poetry to a tissue of conventional religious symbolism, but offers valuable insights into the medieval religious mentality. A full introduction to Chaucer's life and work is Donald A. Howard, *Chaucer: his life, his works, his world* (New York, 1987). Other good general introductions are D. S. Brewer, *Chaucer* (3rd ed., London, 1973), and the same author's *An Introduction to Chaucer* (London, 1984). Chaucer's language is well treated in J. D. Burnley, *A Guide to Chaucer's Language* (Norman OK, 1983).

The best book-length study of Chaucer's poetry in general is still Charles Muscatine, *Chaucer and the French Tradition* (Berkeley CA, 1957); his observations on the implications of contrasts of style and genre among the *Canterbury Tales* are the starting-point for much later work. Good also are Alfred David, *The Strumpet Muse: Art and Morals in Chaucer's Poetry* (Bloomington IN, 1976), and several essay-collections: *Chaucer's Mind and Art*, ed. A. C. Cawley (London, 1969); *Chaucer and Chaucerians: Critical Studies in Middle English Literature*, ed. D. S. Brewer (London, 1966), original essays by well-known scholars; *Geoffrey Chaucer*, ed. D. S. Brewer (in the series *Writers and Their Background*, London, 1974); *Geoffrey Chaucer: A Collection of Original Articles*, ed. George D.

Economou (New York, 1975); *A Companion to Chaucer Studies*, ed. Beryl Rowland (2nd ed., London, 1979); *The Cambridge Chaucer Companion*, ed. Piero Boitani and Jill Mann (Cambridge, 1986).

The fullest critical treatment of the *Canterbury Tales* is Derek Pearsall, *The Canterbury Tales* (London, 1985), with extensive reviews of earlier criticism. Donald Howard, *The Idea of the Canterbury Tales* (Berkeley CA, 1976), suggests several approaches to the question of the poem's unity. Jill Mann, *Chaucer and Medieval Estates Satire* (Cambridge, 1973), shows how Chaucer's treatment of social types extends a long tradition of medieval social satire. V. A. Kolve, *Chaucer and the Imagery of Narrative* (London, 1984), studies the poem in a richly detailed context of medieval visual imagery. The standard collection of source material is *Sources and Analogues of Chaucer's Canterbury Tales*, ed. W. F. Bryan and Germaine Dempster (Chicago, 1941). Larry Benson and Theodore Andersson, eds., *The Literary Context of Chaucer's Fabliaux* (New York, 1971) collects analogues to the tales of the Miller, Reeve, Shipman, and Merchant.

Critical responses to Chaucer's poetry from the fourteenth century to modern times are collected in *Chaucer: The Critical Heritage*, ed. D. S. Brewer (2 vols., London, 1978). Current work on Chaucer is recorded and reviewed in the annual *Studies in the Age of Chaucer* (1979–).

Additional reading

Larry D. Benson, "The Order of the Canterbury Tales," *Studies in the Age of Chaucer* 3 (1981), 77–120.

J. A. Burrow, *Ricardian Poetry: Chaucer, Gower, Langland, and the Gawain Poet* (London, 1971).

Helen Cooper, *The Structure of the Canterbury Tales* (London, 1983).

E. T. Donaldson, *Speaking of Chaucer* (selected essays, London, 1970).

R. W. Hanning, "The Struggle Between Noble Design and Chaos: The Literary Tradition of Chaucer's *Knight's Tale*," *Literary Review* 23 (1980), 519–41.

R. E. Kaske, "The Knight's Interruption of the 'Monk's Tale'," *ELH* 24 (1957), 249–68.

G. L. Kittredge, *Chaucer and His Poetry* (Cambridge MA, 1915).

J. L. Lowes, *Geoffrey Chaucer and the Development of His Genius* (Boston, 1934).

J. M. Manly, *Some New Light on Chaucer* (New York, 1926).

Michio Masui, ed., *A New Rime Index to 'The Canterbury Tales'* (Tokyo, 1988).

Anne Middleton, "The Idea of Public Poetry in the Reign of Richard II," *Speculum* 53 (1978), 94–114.

"War by Other Means: Marriage and Chivalry in Chaucer," *Studies in the Age of Chaucer. Proceedings*, *No. 1* (1984), 119–33.

Lee Patterson, "Chaucerian Confession: Penitential Tradition and the Pardoner," *Medievalia et Humanistica* 7 (1976), 153–73.

" 'For the Wyves Love of Bathe': Feminine Rhetoric and Poetic Resolution in the *Roman de la Rose* and the *Canterbury Tales*," *Speculum* 58 (1983), 656–95.

Negotiating the Past. The Historical Understanding of Medieval Literature (Madison WI, 1987).

D. W. Robertson, Jr., *Chaucer's London* (London, 1968).

Olive Sayce, "Chaucer's 'Retractions': The conclusion of the *Canterbury Tales* and its Place in Literary Tradition," *Medium Aevum* 40 (1971), 230–48.

V. J. Scattergood and J. W. Sherborne, eds., *English Court Culture in the Later Middle Ages* (London, 1983).

Ann Thompson, *Shakespeare's Chaucer* (Liverpool, 1978).

Translations

Nevill Coghill, trans., *The Canterbury Tales* (Harmondsworth, 1952).

Theodore Morrison, trans., *The Portable Chaucer* (2nd ed., New York, 1975).

David Wright, trans., *The Canterbury Tales* (Oxford, 1985).

Recordings

Helge Kökeritz, *Chaucer Readings* (Lexington). Designed for use with Kökeritz's pamphlet, *A Guide to Chaucer's Pronunciation* (New Haven, 1954; rpt. Toronto, 1978).

The General Prologue (complete), read by Nevill Coghill, Norman Davis and John Burrow (Argo).

The Pardoner's Tale and *The Nun's Priest's Tale*, read by Robert Ross (Caedmon).

Chaucer, The General Prologue, read by Paul Piehler; available from Prof. Piehler, Golden Clarioun Literary Services, 2556 Shetland Park, St. Lazare, P.Q., J0P 1V0, Canada.

Index to discussions of individual tales